The A to Z of
Cake
Decorating
Flowers

The A to Z of
Cake
Decorating
Flowers

Lorraine Sorby-Howlett
&
Marian Jones

NEW
HOLLAND

Dedication

We dedicate this book to our ever-patient families and friends who offer us so much encouragement.

Cover: The front arrangement was made up of three different wired sprays using a selection of flowers from the book amongst which was wired delicate bunches of baby's breath. A perspex stand was used to support the centre and top sprays. The front spray is resting on a piece of driftwood. Ribbon loops were used to contrast the colour of the flowers.

Half title: A square cake with curved side embroidery, fine lace around the bottom edge and finished with Royal Bifrenaria Orchids, maidenhair fern and ribbon loops.

Title left: Two-tiered wedding cake with scalloped lace edges around the base of each cake. There is a spray of fairy bells, Mexican orange blossom and jasmine on each tier and the top has a royal icing scroll and rings.

Title right: Carnation (see page 35).

Contents and back cover: Romantic heart-shaped cake with an offset spray of jasmine and baby's breath finished with ribbon loops.

Contents right: Christmas Bush (page 35).

First published in the UK in 1989 by
New Holland (Publishers) Ltd
37 Connaught Street, London W2 2AZ

ISBN 1 85368 087 7

Edited by Carol Jacobson
Text by Lorraine Sorby-Howlett and Marian Jones
Photography by Leonard Osbeck

Typesetting processed by Deblaere Typesetting Pty Ltd
Printed and bound in Hong Kong by Toppan Printing Co. (HK) Ltd

Contents

Elements of a Flower

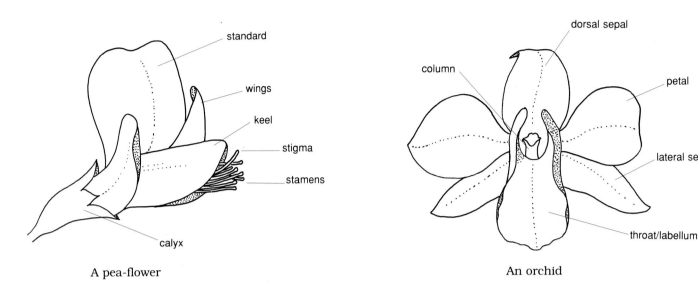

A pea-flower

An orchid

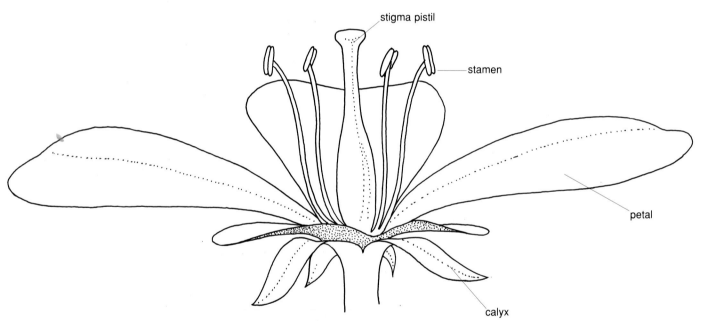

A standard flower

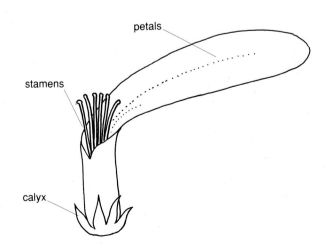

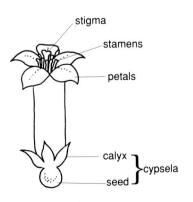

Introduction

As cake decorators we must never lose sight of the fact that we are responsible for an edible product which includes the decorations we add. Because of this, we must not use too many inedible products such as wires, bristles and nylon, etc.

Although we have given instructions to wire many of our flowers, we strongly recommend you omit the wire when decorating a cake and just tape together the stamens. You will still achieve a beautiful and realistic flower.

We have, wherever possible, made each sugarflower for this book from a real one. As you are aware there are many varieties of the same flowers and we have used the one we think would be most suitable for cake decorating. Should you require a particular species not listed then use the same principles and techniques we have described but have the real flower beside you and make any alterations necessary. We have also taken artistic licence with some of our flowers to make them more suitable for use in cake decorating.

Included are several recipes for modelling paste that we have collected over the years. We do not specifically recommend any one of these recipes. You should try them and find the one most suitable for your own use. We have found that climate differences greatly affect the drying and setting of modelling paste.

Marian Jones and Lorraine Sorby-Howlett

Hexagonal cake with a double frill around the base.
The top has a spray of lasiandra osbeckia, sweet blossom and hyacinths.

Step-by-step

Pulled Method

Step 1: Flatten the top of a piece of modelling paste.

Step 2: Using scissors, make the required number of deep cuts into the flattened top.

Step 3: Pull the petals into shape.

Step 4: Push the petals into position.

Step 5: Hollow out the centre with a modelling tool.

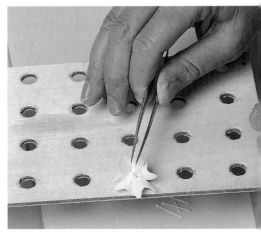

Step 6: Place in a drying stand and insert the required number of stamens into the centre.

Hollow Out and Cut Method

Step 1: Using a modelling tool, hollow out a piece of modelling paste using light pressure against the index finger.

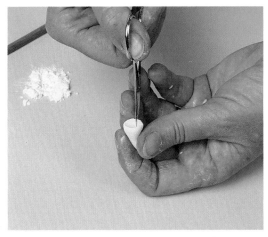

Step 2: Cradle the hollow cone between the thumb and index finger.

Step 3: Make the required number of cuts in the top.

Mitre or Pinch

Using scissors, cut each petal to a point or pinch as shown.

Taping Stamens

Using florists tape, attach the required number of stamens together.

Wiring the Centre

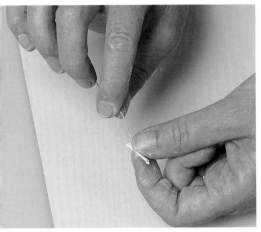

Step 1: Make a hook on a length of wire. Place along stamen cottons.

Step 2: Twist the wire around the ends of the cottons and the hook.

Step 3: Fan out the stamen heads and insert into the centre of the flower.

Hooked Centre

Make a small hook on the end of a length of wire. Place into the centre of the flower and pull through to secure.

Making a Mexican Hat

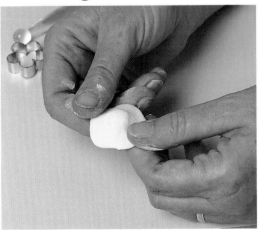

Step 1: Finger the edges of a piece of modelling paste, leaving the centre raised.

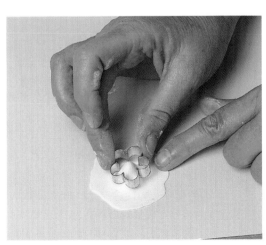

Step 2: Place the cutter over the raised section and cut out the shape.

Bouncing

Place the petal on foam and, using a balling tool, push gently in the centre.

Veining

Place the petal over the desired veiner and press gently.

Balling Up

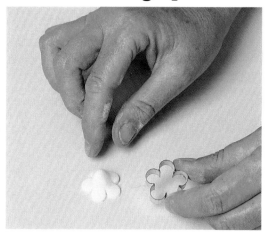

Step 1: Cut out the shape.

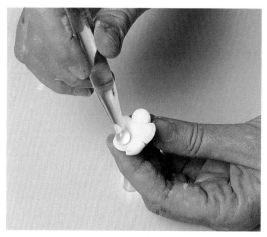

Step 2: Place a balling tool on each petal and, using light pressure, press against the index finger.

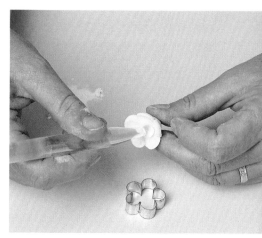

Step 3: Place a balling tool in the centre of the flower and gently push all the petals upwards.

Rolling Out

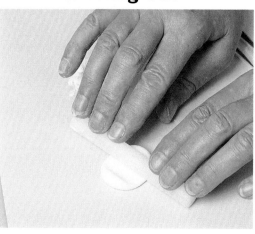

Take a piece of modelling paste and roll out.

Cutting a Pattern

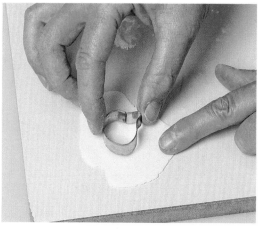

Place the pattern or cutter in position.

Frilling

Using a modelling tool, roll along the edge of the petal.

Twisting the Top

Using the thumb and index finger, gently twist the top edge of the petals.

Pulling from Below

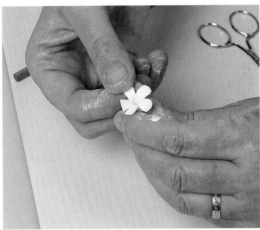

Place the index finger underneath the petal and the thumb on top. Using gentle pressure, pull the petal between the two fingers.

Pulling from Above

Place the thumb underneath the petal and using gentle pressure, pull the petal across the thumb.

Assembly

Step 1: Line a drying stand with foil, wax paper or plastic wrap. Pipe the desired amount of royal icing into the base.

Step 2: Position the petals into the royal icing.

Step 3: Using pointed tweezers, insert the stamens to cover the royal icing.

Colouring

Step 1: An air-brush may be used to colour the petals.

Step 2: Brush with chalk dust or use diluted food colouring.

Sizes and Patterns

Wires used throughout the book

Fine—0.2 mm (008 inch)
Medium—0.3 mm (012 inch)
Heavy—0.4 mm (0159 inch)

Modelling paste pieces used for the flowers

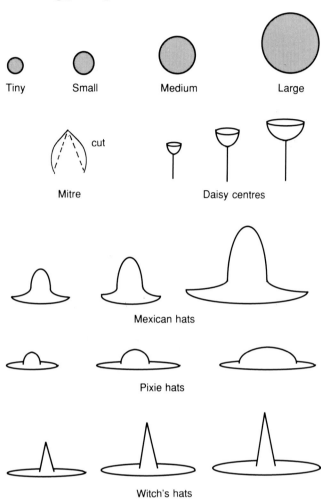

Miniature Leaf

Secure a small piece of modelling paste on the end of a stamen. To shape, pull the top and flatten the sides with the fingers. Vein.

Jasmine Leaf

Take a small piece of modelling paste and insert a fine wire or stamen. Roll between the fingers to lengthen. Pinch the top and place on a board and flatten. Make a single vein up the centre. Drape to dry.

Banksia Leaf

Roll out a piece of modelling paste and cut out a leaf shape using the rounded end of a rose petal cutter. Serrate the edge. Drape and allow to dry.

Tendrils

Twist a length of fine gauge green wire around a cocktail stick.

Phyllodes

A flattened piece serving the function of a leaf but without a blade.

Leaf Patterns

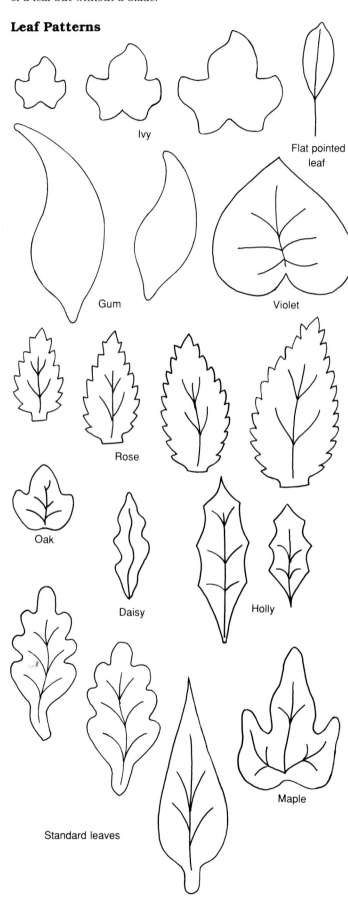

Recipes

Modelling Paste No. 1

Half Mix
1 teaspoon powdered gelatine
1 teaspoon powdered glucose
6 teaspoons (30 ml/1 fl oz) water
1 ½ cups (250 g/8 oz) icing (confectioners) sugar, sifted

Full Mix
2 teaspoons powdered gelatine
2 teaspoons powdered glucose
¼ cup (50 ml/2 fl oz) water
3 cups (500 g/1 lb) icing (confectioners) sugar, sifted

Soak the gelatine and glucose in the water for 15–20 minutes then dissolve completely over low heat. Add to the icing sugar and mix well to a smooth pliable consistency. Add more icing sugar if necessary until the required consistency is reached. Store in a plastic bag in a sealed container. Allow to rest for 30 minutes before using.

Modelling Paste No. 2

2 level teaspoons powdered gelatine
1 level teaspoon liquid glucose
6 teaspoons (30 ml/1 fl oz) cold water
1 ¾ cups (300 g/10 oz) icing (confectioners) sugar, sifted
1 level teaspoon gum tragacanth compound

Soak the gelatine and glucose in the water for 30 minutes then dissolve completely over low heat. Add half the icing sugar to the gum compound then add the gelatine mixture. Mix well. Gradually add the remaining icing sugar until the mixture is smooth and pliable. Store in a plastic bag in a sealed container. Allow to rest for 30 minutes before using.

Modelling Paste No. 3

Microwave method
4 teaspoons powdered gelatine
¼ (50 ml/2 fl oz) water
2 teaspoons liquid glucose
3 cups (500 g/1 lb) icing (confectioners) sugar, sifted
1 ½-2 level teaspoons pure gum tragacanth

Pour the water into a glass container and sprinkle in the gelatine. Allow to stand for at least 15 minutes. Place in a microwave oven and heat gently on medium–low setting for 15 seconds until lukewarm and the gelatine is dissolved. Remove from the oven, add the glucose and stir until completely dissolved. Rewarm for a few seconds in the microwave if necessary. Add the liquid to the icing sugar and gum tragacanth. Mix well until the mixture is smooth and pliable. Store in a plastic bag in a sealed container. Allow to rest for 1 hour before using.
Note: If in a hurry place the paste in a freezer for 10 minutes.

Pettinice Paste

2 teaspoons pure gum tragacanth
500 g (1 lb) Pettinice (commercial plastic icing)
1 teaspoon eggwhite

Knead the gum tragacanth into the Pettinice and then add the eggwhite. Knead well. Allow to stand for 24 hours before using. Knead again before use.

Heated Copha Paste

2 teaspoons (10 ml) powdered gelatine
6 teaspoons (30 ml/1 fl oz) water
3 cups (500 g/1 lb) icing (confectioners) sugar, sifted
3 teaspoons pure gum tragacanth
2 tablespoons (40 ml) eggwhite
40 g (1 ¼ oz) Copha (solid white vegetable shortening), softened

Soak the gelatine in the water for 30 minutes. Sift half the icing sugar with the gum tragacanth and warm gently in the oven. Gently heat the gelatine and water mixture until completely dissolved. Add to the heated icing sugar together with the eggwhite. Gradually add the remaining icing sugar until the mixture is smooth and pliable. Knead the softened Copha through the mixture. Allow to stand at least 24 hours before using.

Royal Icing No. 1

1 medium eggwhite at room temperature
1 ½ cups (250 g/8 oz) icing (confectioners) sugar, sifted
2 drops acetic acid, optional

Place the eggwhite in a bowl and beat gently to break up. Gradually add the icing sugar, one spoonful at a time, beating well after each addition. Continue in this manner until the mixture is thickened. Add the acetic acid (if used) and mix well. Continue to add the icing sugar until desired peak is reached.

Royal Icing No. 2

1 teaspoon actiwhite or egg powder
1 tablespoon (20 ml) cold water
¾ cup (125 g/4 oz) icing (confectioners) sugar, sifted
2 drops acetic acid, optional

Dissolve the actiwhite or egg powder in the water for 15 minutes. Stir gently then strain through a fine strainer into a mixing bowl. Add the icing sugar, one spoonful at a time until the mixture starts to thicken. Add the acetic acid (if used). Continue to add the icing sugar until the required peak is reached.
Note: An electric mixer may be used but be careful not to overbeat.

Gum Glue

1 teaspoon gum arabic
3 teaspoons (15 ml) hot water
½ teaspoon (2.5 ml) pure alcohol

Dissolve the gum arabic in the hot water then add the alcohol. Allow to cool. Store in a sealed container.

Leaf Shine

3 teaspoons gum arabic
3 teaspoons (15 ml) hot water

Dissolve the gum arabic in the hot water. Apply to leaves or petals while hot. Store in a sealed container and reheat in the microwave before reusing.

Alcohol Wash

Place a few drops of liquid food colour in a small container. Add 3–4 drops of cold water then dilute with pure alcohol until the desired colour.

Pollen

Mix powdered gelatine and powdered chalk together. Store in a sealed container.

Coloured Sugar

Mix caster (super fine) sugar and powdered chalk together. Store in a sealed container.

Edible Glitter

60 g (2 oz) gum arabic
2 tablespoons water

Dissolve the gum arabic in the water. Strain if necessary and brush onto a clean baking tray. Place in a 140°C (275°F/Gas 1) oven until dry. Scrape off the tray with a knife then flake between the fingers and store in an airtight container.

Hints

Remember you are working with a food product and therefore you should use only edible products, especially colourings. **Note:** Non-toxic does **not** mean edible.

Rest your modelling paste after mixing by placing in a freezer for 10 minutes.

Modelling paste can be stored in small containers in a freezer until needed.

Use any leftover paste to make modelling stands that you might not have readily available.

Flowers are more lifelike if made in white paste and shaded when dry.

Keep a spare modelling paste petal, dried, for use as a colour tester when air-brushing.

If left to stand for 24 hours after separating the egg, eggwhite will make a stronger icing.

Keep all equipment spotlessly clean. Any mark or tiny piece of sugar grit shows on your petals.

If your hands are cold wipe a small amount of Copha (solid white shortening) on the fingers while making flowers.

A cornflour (cornstarch) box is very useful for supporting petals while drying.

Cornflour (cornstarch) in a fine mesh (muslin) bag is very handy when shaking a small amount on the hands or work surface.

Potato flour mixed with cornflour (cornstarch) makes a finer mix than pure cornflour.

To dry corn silks for use as stamens, spread on a tray and place in fan-forced oven for 30 minutes on a very low temperature 100°C (200°F/Gas On) then wrap in a paper towel and store in a dry box.

Runny royal or royal icing thinned down is very handy for making small buds. Dip the stamen head into runny royal and allow to dry.

For a realistic flower centre, tied corn silks can be painted or air-brushed to colour. Lightly brush the tips with eggwhite and dip into coloured pollen.

For a heavy, more lifelike stamen for a larger flower, dip the stamen head in eggwhite and then into coloured pollen.

If colours have a tendency to curdle when mixing with a spirit (e.g. alcohol) add 1–2 drops of water **before** the addition of the spirit.

If pure alcohol is unobtainable use neat vodka.

The Flowers

Flowers and patterns are shown as close as possible to actual size. We have not stated the number of stamens to insert where a particular flower has a varied amount. You may insert the number that suits your flower.

Abelia

Abelia spp.

Colours: pink

Pulled method

Step 1: Tape fine stamens to a length of medium gauge wire.

Step 2: Colour modelling paste to the desired shade.

Step 3: Take a medium-sized ball of modelling paste, roll to a teardrop shape, flatten the top and hollow out. Make five evenly spaced cuts around the top (1).

Step 4: Pull each petal from underneath.

Step 5: Press each petal to thin out.

Step 6: Place a grooved modelling tool into the centre and gently press the flower onto it.

Step 7: Remove the tool and insert the wired stamens (2).

Step 8: Gently turn each petal outwards. Allow to dry.

Step 9: Paint the back of the flower with a deeper pink colour.

Step 10: Attach or paint a small calyx to the back of the flower.

African Violet

Saintpaulia spp.

Colours: purple, pink, white

Method 1

Step 1: Tape fine stamens to a length of medium gauge wire.

Step 2: Take a piece of modelling paste and roll out thinly. Using pattern (1), cut out the inner petals and lightly frill the edges.

Step 3: Moisten the stamens and secure the frilled shape tightly around them. Allow to dry.

Step 4: Take a piece of modelling paste and roll out thinly. Using pattern (2), cut out the outer petals and frill the edges.

Step 5: Dampen the back of the dry centre and push into the frilled outer petals. Allow to dry. Colour to suit.

African Violet

Saintpaulia spp.

Colours: purple, pink, white

Pulled method

Step 1: Take a medium-sized ball of modelling paste and flatten the top. Using pattern (1), make five cuts around the top.

Step 2: Pull each section to form a petal shape (2). Thin and frill the edges.

Step 3: Push a grooved modelling tool into the centre and insert a length of medium gauge hooked wire.

Step 4: Add two large yellow stamen heads into the flower centre. Allow to dry.

Agapanthus

Agapanthus spp.

Colours: blue, white

Cutter method

Step 1: Tape a bunch of stamens to a length of medium gauge wire.

Step 2: Take a medium-sized ball of modelling paste, hollow out and make six evenly spaced cuts around the top (1).

Step 3: Mitre each petal then press firmly with the thumb and index finger to remove the cut look.

Step 4: Vein the centre of each petal then insert a modelling tool into the centre to reshape.

Step 5: Insert the wired stamens and allow to dry.

Step 6: Make buds by inserting a length of medium gauge hooked wire into a long piece of modelling paste and groove up the sides.

Step 7: Colour as desired.

Allamanda (Golden Trumpets)

Allamanda spp.

Colours: lemon

Pulled method

Step 1: Colour modelling paste bright golden yellow.

Step 2: Take a medium-sized ball of modelling paste and make a pixie hat (see page 12).

Step 3: Using cutter (1), cut out shape.

Step 4: Hollow out using a pointed modelling tool.

Step 5: Pull the petals to thin out then vein each petal lightly.

Step 6: Turn the top two petals well back.

Step 7: Insert a length of medium gauge wire through the centre of the flower. Allow to dry.

Step 8: Take a tiny ball of green modelling paste for the calyx and push firmly onto the back of the trumpet.

Anemone

Anemone spp.

Colours: various

Step 1: Make a large black daisy centre (see page 12).

Step 2: Take a piece of modelling paste and roll out thinly. Using pattern (1), cut six petals.

Step 3: Finger the edges and frill the top edge.

Step 4: Place on foam and, using a balling tool, cup up gently. Allow to dry.

Step 5: Paint carefully leaving a white area at the bottom of the petal. Allow to dry.

Step 6: Assemble in a shallow patty pan in a small amount of royal icing.

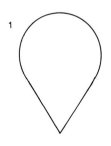

17

Anthurium

Anthurium spp.

Colours: white, pink, red

Step 1: Take a piece of modelling paste and roll out thinly. Using pattern (1), cut out the flower shape.

Step 2: Vein as shown (1).

Step 3: Pierce a hole large enough to take the wire of the spadix. Drape over a cotton ball or in a cornflour (cornstarch) box to dry.

Step 4: To make the spadix take a roll of yellow modelling paste two-thirds the length of the petal (2), insert a length of medium gauge wire, curve slightly and allow to dry.

Step 5: Lightly moisten the spadix with a damp paint brush and coat with a mixture of yellow chalk and fine sugar.

Step 6: Paint or chalk the petals before glazing with hot leaf shine.

Step 7: Attach the spadix with a little royal icing if necessary.

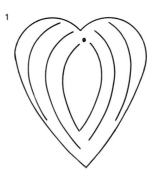

Apple Blossom

Malus putnila spp.

Colours: pink, white

Step 1: Tape several small-headed stamens to a length of medium-gauge wire.

Step 2: Take a medium-sized ball of modelling paste, hollow out and make five evenly spaced cuts around the top (1).

Step 3: Frill each petal and place on foam. Using a balling tool, bounce gently to cup.

Step 4: Dampen the centre and insert the stamens.

Step 5: Remove the excess paste from the back of the flower.

Step 6: Paint or make a small calyx to finish the flower.

Azalea

Azalea spp.

Colours: various

Step 1: Attach one long stamen and then shorter stamens to a length of medium gauge wire.

Step 2: Colour a piece of modelling paste and roll out thinly.

Step 3: Using pattern (1), cut five petals. Keep the petals covered to prevent them drying out.

Step 4: Vein each petal and lightly flute the edges.

Step 5: Turn each petal over and pinch down the backs for two-thirds of the length of the petals. Keep the petals covered to prevent them drying out.

Step 6: Place the first petal in a deep drying stand lined with plastic wrap. Place the second petal to the right of the first petal and the third petal to the left. Place the fourth petal to the right then the fifth petal on top as shown (2).

Step 7: Push the wired stamens through the centre. If necessary, remove the flower in the plastic wrap from the stand and gently secure the flower to the stamens. Allow to dry.

Step 8: Take a piece of modelling paste and colour it green. Using pattern (3), cut out the calyx. Moisten and attach to the flower.

Step 9: Give the flower an overall wash of colour, if necessary, and paint spots on the lower petal to complete.

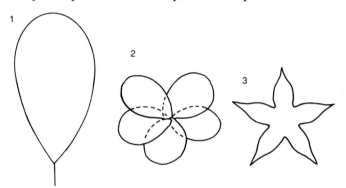

Azalea, Kurume

Azalea kurume

Colours: various

Pulled method

Step 1: Attach fine stamens to a length of medium-gauge wire.

Step 2: Take a medium-sized ball of modelling paste and hollow out (1).

Step 3: Make five evenly spaced shallow cuts around the top.

Step 4: Gently pull each section to form a petal then press firmly to flatten and thin.

Step 5: Insert a modelling tool into the centre to reshape the bell.

Step 6: Add the wired stamens and firmly attach the flower to the wire (2).

Step 7: Twist the petal tops and allow to dry.

Step 8: Colour as desired.

Step 9: To make the bud, attach a medium-sized ball of modelling paste to a length of medium gauge wire. Mark five evenly spaced grooves around the paste to represent the petals.

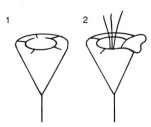

Baby Blue Eyes

Nemophila spp.

Colours: blue

Step 1: Attach some fine stamens to a length of medium gauge wire.

Step 2: Take a medium-sized ball of modelling paste and make a Mexican hat (see page 12). Using pattern (1), cut out the flower.

Step 3: Finger the edges of each petal. Vein and twist the top of the petals.

Step 4: Insert the stamens into the dampened centre of the flower and attach firmly. Allow to dry before painting.

1

Baby's Breath

Gypsophila spp.

Colours: white, cream

Alternate method

Step 1: Take several stems of real baby's breath. Remove the flower heads from the stems and allow the stems to dry for several days.

Step 2: Fill a paper piping bag with soft royal icing and snip a tiny hole in the end. Pipe small dots on the end of each stem. Allow to dry.

Baby's Breath

Gypsophila spp.

Colours: white, cream

Step 1: Take a piece of modelling paste and roll out thinly. Using pattern or cutter (1), cut out no more than six flowers at a time.

Step 2: Dampen the end of a fine stamen and push into one flower. Repeat for the remaining flowers.

Step 3: Gently firm onto the stamen. Allow to dry.

Step 4: Continue in this manner until you complete the required amount of flowers.

1

Banksia

Banksia spp.

Colours: cream, yellow, orange

Step 1: Hook a length of heavy gauge wire.

Step 2: Attach a piece of modelling paste, approximately one-third the length of the finished flower, to the wire.

Step 3: Insert stamens into the top of the paste gradually rounding off the head (1).

Step 4: Continue inserting stamens until the modelling paste is completely covered.

Step 5: Thread another piece of paste, again one-third the length, onto the wire and completely cover with stamens.

Step 6: Repeat step 5. Allow to dry.

Step 7: Finish off with banksia leaves (2).

1

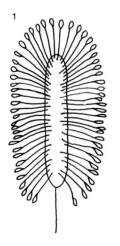

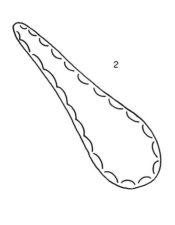

2

Bauera

Rubioides spp.

Colours: pink

Cutter method

Step 1: Take a small ball of modelling paste and attach to a length of medium gauge hooked wire to make the flower centre. Allow to dry.

Step 2: Dampen with eggwhite or gum glue and cover with yellow pollen.

Step 3: Take a piece of modelling paste and roll out thinly. Using pattern (1), cut out the flower.

Step 4: Place on foam and ball each petal. Turn over and bounce gently in the middle.

Step 5: Dampen the back of the centre and push into the petals, attaching firmly. Allow to dry.

Beauty Bush

Kolkwitza spp.

Colours: pink

Pulled method

Step 1: Tape fine yellow stamens to a length of medium gauge wire.

Step 2: Take a medium-sized ball of modelling paste and roll into a teardrop shape. Flatten the top.

Step 3: Hollow out a cone and make five evenly spaced cuts around the top (1).

Step 4: Pull each section from underneath to form petals (2).

Step 5: Press each petal gently to thin out.

Step 6: Push a modelling tool into the centre to reshape.

Step 7: Insert the wired stamens.

Step 8: Gently turn four petals outward, leaving the remaining one flat. Allow to dry.

Step 9: Paint the back of the flower pale pink.

Step 10: Paint orange spots on the front of the flat petal (3).

Begonia

Begonia spp.

Colours: various

Step 1: Form a flat piece of modelling paste on a length of medium gauge wire (1).

Step 2: Moisten with eggwhite and dip in coloured gelatine. Allow to dry.

Step 3: Take a piece of modelling paste and roll out thinly. Using pattern (2), cut one petal and bounce the back on foam. Moisten and attach to the centre.

Step 4: Take a piece of modelling paste and roll out thinly. Using pattern (3), cut one piece and gently frill the edge. Moisten and attach to the centre. Allow to dry before painting.

Step 5: To make the buds, take a medium-sized ball of modelling paste and place on a length of medium gauge wire. Pinch to shape three petals.

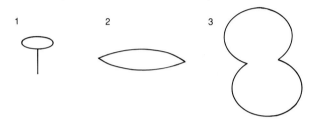

Black Eyed Susan

Rudbeckia spp.

Colours: orange

Step 1: Attach a small ball of modelling paste to a length of medium gauge wire. Paint with eggwhite and dip into coloured gelatine. Allow to completely dry before proceeding with the flower.

Step 2: Take a piece of orange modelling paste and roll out thinly. Using pattern (1), cut out the flower.

Step 3: Finger the edges and turn back the tip of each petal.

Step 4: Attach the dry centre to the flower using a small amount of eggwhite.

Step 5: Using a small balling tool, gently ball each petal towards the centre. Allow to dry.

Step 6: Take a piece of green modelling paste and roll out thinly. Using pattern (2), cut a calyx. Finger the edges. Dampen with eggwhite and attach to the back of the flower. Allow to dry.

Blossom, Double

Colours: pastel shades

Step 1: Tape fine stamens or corn silks to a length of medium gauge wire.

Step 2: Take a piece of modelling paste and roll out thinly. Using pattern (1), cut out a calyx. Moisten and set in a shallow drying stand.

Step 3: Take a piece of modelling paste and roll out thinly. Using pattern (2), cut one shape. Frill the petals and place on the moistened calyx.

Step 4: Take a piece of modelling paste and roll out thinly. Using pattern (3), cut one shape Frill the edges and place on foam. Using a balling tool in the centre, cup the petals.

Step 5: Moisten the back of the petals and place in position on top of the first row of petals.

Step 6: Pull the stamen through the centre. Allow to dry.

Blossom, Sweet

Colours: various

Cutter method

Step 1: Take a small ball of modelling paste and make a Mexican hat (see page 12). Using cutter (1), cut out the flower shape.

Step 2: Insert a length of medium gauge wire.

Step 3: Using a medium balling tool, press into each petal to cup the centre and thin the edges.

Step 4: Insert fine stamens and allow to dry.

Step 5: Colour as desired, painting a small green calyx on the back of the flower.

Step 6: To make the bud, attach a small piece of modelling paste to a length of medium gauge wire. Mark five grooves and twist to dry before colouring.

24

Blue Butterfly Bush

Psoralea spp.

Colours: various

Cutter method

Step 1: Curve over the finger one long and four shorter stamens.

Step 2: Take a piece of modelling paste and roll out thinly. Using cutter (1), cut two pieces and make a cut as marked on the diagram.

Step 3: Smooth the edges and place on foam. Gently ball, taking care to reverse the pattern on the second piece.

Step 4: Allow to dry in a curved drying stand.

Step 5: Take a piece of modelling paste and roll out thinly. Using pattern (2), cut one front petal.

Step 6: Using a small balling tool, pull towards the narrow end. Allow to dry.

Step 7: Paint the front petal. Allow to dry.

Step 8: Assemble the petals in a shallow pan using a small amount of royal icing and then insert the stamens. Lastly add the front petals.

Step 9: When dry add small wired calyx to the back of the flower.

Blueberry Ash

Elaeocarpus spp.

Colours: pink, white

Pulled method

Step 1: Take a small ball of white modelling paste and hollow out the centre (1).

Step 2: Make six very shallow evenly spaced cuts around the top (2).

Step 3: Flatten and slightly pull each section to form petals. Turn each one well back.

Step 4: Insert the round end of a modelling tool and round off the base of the flowers.

Step 5: Insert a length of fine gauge hooked wire. Allow to dry.

Step 6: Paint a small green spot on the back of each petal and paint a calyx on the base.

Step 7: To make the bud, take a small ball of modelling paste and mould onto a length of fine gauge hooked wire.

Step 8: Make four indents in the top and paint a calyx.

Boronia, Brown

Boronia spp.

Colours: yellow/brown

Step 1: Take a tiny ball of yellow modelling paste and shape into a teardrop.

Step 2: Using a sharp craft knife, make two deep cuts in the shape of a cross (1).

Step 3: Using a pointed modelling tool, place in the centre of the cut and gently pull each petal across your index finger (2, 3).

Step 4: Moisten the head of a stamen or fine knotted wire and insert into the centre of the flower.

Step 5: Using a small balling tool, gently cup each petal towards the centre (4). Allow to dry.

Step 6: Paint the back of the flower with brown colouring.

Step 7: To make buds, take a tiny ball of yellow modelling paste and attach to lengths of fine gauge knotted wire. Make four cuts around bud using the back of a knife (5). Allow to dry before painting with brown colouring. Do not paint in the grooves.

Boronia, Pink

Boronia spp.

Colours: pink

Step 1: Take a small ball of pink modelling paste and hollow out the centre. Make four evenly spaced cuts around the top (1). Mitre each petal.

Step 2: Insert a length of fine gauge wire into the centre and cup the petals, using a fine modelling tool.

Step 3: Insert a thick yellow stamen.

Step 4: Allow to dry before painting the back of flower a deeper shade of pink.

Bottlebrush

Callistemon spp.

Colours: red, lemon, crimson, white, purple

Step 1: Make the bract centres by winding sewing thread over your fingers until the required thickness. Secure with a length of fine gauge wire through the centre (1). You will need 50–60 bracts to complete the flower, depending on the size required.

Step 2: Take a tiny ball of green modelling paste and hollow out to form a cup. Moisten the centre and insert a wired thread. Continue until all the bracts are completed. Allow to dry.

Step 3: Cut the threads and trim to neaten (2).

Step 4: Paint the tips of each thread with eggwhite, then dip into yellow pollen. Allow to dry.

Step 5: Wire all the bracts together to form the flower head.

Bougainvillea

Bougainvillea spp.

Colours: various

Cutter method

Step 1: To make the centre flowers, take a tiny ball of modelling paste and shape into a teardrop.

Step 2: Using a sharp craft knife, make two deep cuts in the top in the shape of a cross.

Step 3: Place a pointed modelling tool in middle of the cut and gently pull each petal across your index finger to lengthen.

Step 4: Moisten the head of a stamen and insert into the flower centre. Allow to dry.

Step 5: Take a medium-sized ball of modelling paste and make a Mexican hat (see page 12). Using pattern (1), cut one shape.

Step 6: Finger the edges to thin, then vein.

Step 7: Firm the flower onto a length of medium gauge hooked wire, pushing the petals towards the centre.

Step 8: Insert one to three small flowers and some thick stamens into the centre.

 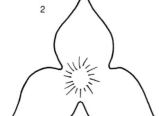

Bouvardia

Bouvardia spp.

Colours: pink, white

Step 1: Take a tiny ball of pink modelling paste and hollow out (1).

Step 2: Make four evenly spaced cuts around the top and mitre each petal (2).

Step 3: Press each petal gently with a modelling tool to soften the cut edges (3).

Step 4: Insert a length of fine gauge hooked wire. Allow to dry.

Broom

Viminaria spp.

Colours: lemon

Cutter method

Step 1: To make the pea centre, attach a small ball of lemon modelling paste to a length of medium gauge hooked wire. Flatten and bend slightly backwards (1). Allow to dry.

Step 2: Take a piece of modelling paste and roll out thinly. Using pattern (2), cut one shape. Thin and slightly frill the edges. Moisten and attach to the pea centre. Allow to dry.

Step 3: Using pale green modelling paste, cut a thin strip (3) to form the wings. Moisten and attach at the back of the pea centre. Allow to dry.

Step 4: Take a piece of modelling paste and roll out thinly. Using pattern (4), cut one piece. Thin and slightly frill the edges. Pinch the centre to mark.

Step 5: Moisten and attach to the centre of the flower, bending this petal slightly backwards.

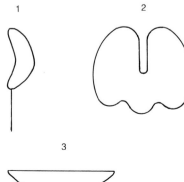 

Browallia

Streptosolen spp.

Colours: orange, lemon

Step 1: Take a medium-sized ball of yellow modelling paste, flatten the top and make five cuts around the top (1).

Step 2: Pull each section to form petals (2). Thin and frill the edges and vein each petal using a cocktail stick.

Step 3: Push a grooved modelling tool into the centre and insert a length of medium gauge hooked wire.

Step 4: Push two short yellow stamens into the centre. Allow to dry.

Step 5: Paint the petals orange and leave the centre yellow. Allow to dry.

Brunfelsia

Brunfelsia spp.

Colours: lemon

Cutter method

Step 1: Take a large ball of yellow modelling paste and make a Mexican hat (see page 12).

Step 2: Using cutter (1) cut out the flower. Lengthen the top petal slightly by cutting on either side.

Step 3: Lightly frill each petal and ball the top petal on foam. Turn it towards the centre leaving the other petals flat.

Step 4: Insert a large stamen or small daisy centre well down into the centre of the flower. Allow to dry.

Bulbine

Bulbine spp.

Colours: lemon

Cutter method

Step 1: Tape several small-headed stamens to a length of medium gauge wire.

Step 2: Take a piece of modelling paste and roll out thinly. Using cutter (1), cut one piece.

Step 3: Finger each petal and pinch the top edge.

Step 4: Insert the wired stamens into the flower centre and attach firmly.

Buttercup

Ranunculus spp.

Colours: yellow

Step 1: Take a piece of yellow modelling paste and make a Mexican hat (see page 12). Using either cutter (1), cut one flower depending on the size required.

Step 2: Using a balling tool, cup each petal, place on foam and bounce with a large balling tool in the centre.

Step 3: Insert a length of medium gauge wire through the back of the flower and secure.

Step 4: Insert 8–10 small-headed yellow stamens into the flower centre. Allow to dry.

Step 5: Paint with leaf shine.

Cactus Flower

Colours: various

Step 1: Take a medium-sized ball of modelling paste and make a Mexican hat (see page 12). Using pattern (1), cut one piece.

Step 2: Place on foam and, using a balling tool, gently stroke each petal towards the centre

Step 3: Insert a large-headed stamen. Allow to dry.

Step 4: Take a piece of modelling paste and roll out thinly. Using pattern (2), cut and vein three petals.

Step 5: Place a piece of foil over a 5 cm (2 inch) curtain ring and place the petals in position (3).

Step 6: Repeat step 4. Moisten the back and place these petals in between the back petals. Allow to dry.

Step 7: Attach the dry centre to the base petals with a little royal icing. Allow to dry.

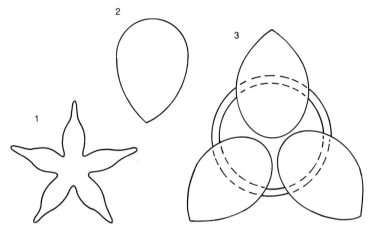

Camellia

Camellia spp.

Colours: various

Step 1: Take a medium-sized ball of modelling paste and shape into a long cone (1).

Step 2: Take a piece of modelling paste and roll out thinly. Using pattern (2), cut three or four petals to fit tightly around the centre. Trim the cone and allow to dry.

Step 3: Take a piece of modelling paste and roll out thinly. Again using pattern (2), cut eight petals and finger the edges. Turn backwards, dampen and place in a circle in a drying stand to form the outer petals.

Step 4: Cut a further seven petals using pattern (2), dampen and place in position to form a second row.

Step 5: Again cut six more petals using pattern (2), dampen and place in position for the third row.

Step 6: For the last row make four petals (2), dampen and place in position.

Step 7: Dampen the base of the dry centre and push firmly into the centre of the flower. Allow to dry.

Carnation

Dianthus spp.

Colours: various

Step 1: Take a piece of modelling paste and roll out thinly. Using cutter (1), cut out shape.

Step 2: Using a craft tool, make fine cuts around the edge.

Step 3: Using a fine modelling tool, frill the edge. Moisten, fold in half and pleat together (2). Attach to a length of medium gauge wire and allow to dry.

Step 4: Add two more shapes (3), cutting and frilling each before attaching to the centre. Allow each one to dry before adding the next one.

Step 5: Cut one more shape (1). Cut, frill and attach to the centre.

Step 6: Take a ball of green modelling paste and make a Mexican hat (see page 12). Using pattern (4), cut out the calyx. Hollow out, moisten and attach to the flower.

Step 7: Using sharp scissors, cut small V-shaped cuts around the base of calyx (5). Allow to dry.

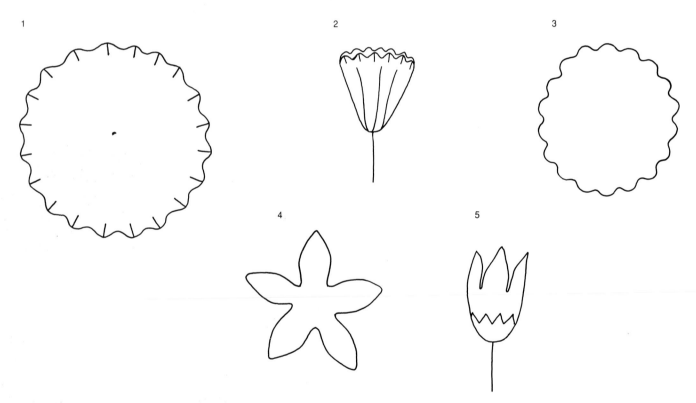

Carnation, Pixie

Dianthus spp.

Colours: various

Step 1: Take a piece of modelling paste and roll out thinly. Using pattern (1), cut one shape.

Step 2: Using a craft tool, make fine cuts around the edge. Frill with a fine modelling tool and place in a small drying stand.

Step 3: Cut two more shapes (1) and repeat the cutting and frilling. Attach one on top of the other and then attach to the one already in the drying stand.

Step 4: Cut one more shape (1) and repeat the cutting and frilling. Moisten the centre and fold in half and then in half again (2). Moisten the back and push into the centre of the completed petals.

Step 5: Arrange the centre to suit the flower and allow to dry. Colour as desired.

Step 6: Take a medium-sized ball of modelling paste and make a Mexican hat (see page 12). Using pattern (3), cut out a calyx. Hollow out, moisten and attach to the back of the dry flower.

Step 7: Using sharp scissors cut small V-shaped cuts around the base of the calyx (4).

Cathedral Bells

Cobea spp.

Colours: white, green, lilac

Step 1: Tape together 8–10 fine stamens and attach to a length of medium gauge wire.

Step 2: Take a large ball of modelling paste, hollow out and frill the top edge (1).

Step 3: Insert the stamens and allow to dry.

Step 4: Take a piece of green modelling paste and roll out thinly. Using pattern (2), cut out the calyx.

Step 5: Lightly frill the edges of the petals.

Step 6: Moisten the calyx and attach to the back of the flower.

Cherry Blossom

Prunus spp.

Colours: pink, white

Cutter method

Step 1: Tape several small-headed stamens to a length of medium gauge wire.

Step 2: Take a piece of modelling paste and roll out thinly. Using cutter (1), cut two shapes.

Step 3: Take one shape for the inside row, frill the petals and place on foam. Using a small balling tool, cup each petal. Set aside.

Step 4: Take the second shape and frill the petals. Dampen the centre and place the first shape inside the second.

Step 5: Put the flower onto foam and firmly press in the centre with a medium balling tool.

Step 6: Dampen the centre and insert the wired stamens. Rearrange the petals if necessary.

Christmas Bells

Alstroemeria spp.

Colours: red, orange

Cutter method

Step 1: Tape together six fine-headed stamens and attach to a length of heavy gauge wire.

Step 2: Take a medium-sized ball of yellow or orange modelling paste, hollow out and make six shallow cuts on the top.

Step 3: Pull each petal slightly or mitre then insert a modelling tool to reshape the bell.

Step 4: Insert the stamens so that the heads are level with the end of the bell (1).

Step 5: Allow to completely dry before painting the backs of the flowers with scarlet or burgundy food colouring. Leave a small area around the edge of the bell unpainted.

Step 6: To make the bud, take a medium ball of modelling paste and attach to a length of medium gauge wire. Roll into a log shape. Gently bend and make six grooves in the tip. Paint the base green and the tip red.

Christmas Bush

Ceratopetalum spp.

Colours: pinkish red

Cutter method

Step 1: Wire a bunch of fine cottons with a length of medium gauge wire.

Step 2: Take a small ball of white modelling paste, hollow out into a narrow cone and make five evenly spaced cuts around the top (1).

Step 3: Insert the wired cottons into the centre of the flower.

Step 4: Using scissors, mitre each petal, roll and thin.

Step 5: Mix together red, orange and a touch of blue to colour the flower.

1

Chrysanthemum

Chrysanthemum X

Colours: various

Step 1: Attach a tiny ball of modelling paste to a length of heavy gauge wire. Moisten and cover with yellow pollen. Allow to dry.

Step 2: Take a piece of modelling paste and roll out thinly. Using pattern (1), cut two shapes. Place each shape on foam and use a balling tool in the centre to cup. Moisten the centre and attach one shape then the other to the centre ball. Allow to dry.

Step 3: Take a piece of modelling paste and roll out thinly. Using pattern (2), cut three shapes. Place on foam and using a balling tool, pull each petal towards the centre.

Step 4: Lay these pieces on top of each other with a small amount of eggwhite in between and the petals alternating.

Step 5: Using pattern (3), cut two shapes and ball the petals as before. Place in position on the other petals.

Step 6: Using pattern (4), cut two shapes and ball the petals. Place in position on the other petals.

Step 7: Moisten the back of the dry centre and pull into position through the other petals.

Step 8: Place on a narrow drying stand made from 1.25 cm (1/2 inch) pipe set in a firm base (5). Allow to dry.

Step 9: To make the bud, repeat steps 1 and 2, adding a small calyx.

3

4

5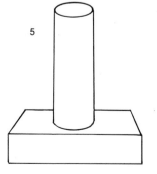

Cistus

Cistus X

Colours: white/pink, red, orange/purple

Step 1: Using medium gauge wire, wire together one small daisy centre (see page 12) and some corn silks.

Step 2: Take a piece of green modelling paste and roll out thinly. Using pattern (1), cut out a calyx and place in a drying stand.

Step 3: Take a piece of modelling paste and roll out thinly. Using pattern (2), cut five petals and frill the edges of each one.

Step 4: Dampen the calyx and arrange the petals in it, overlapping each one.

Step 5: Insert the wired centre. Allow to dry in a drying rack.

Clerodendrum Tomentosum (seed pod)

Clerodendrum spp.

Colours: brown, red

Cutter method

Step 1: Take some dark brown sewing thread and wrap around your finger approximately thirty times. Place a length of heavy gauge wire in the centre and twist to secure. Cut the cotton loops with scissors and fan out.

Step 2: Take a piece of green modelling paste and roll out thinly. Using pattern (1), cut a small green calyx and place in a drying stand.

Step 3: Take a piece of brown modelling paste and roll out thinly. Using cutter (2), cut one shape.

Step 4: Finger the edges and vein. Place on foam and curve the petals with a balling tool.

Step 5: Dampen the calyx and place the pod in position.

Step 6: Insert the wired cotton into the pod and calyx and secure.

Step 7: Make six seeds from tiny balls of red/orange modelling paste. Attach with royal icing or gum arabic solution. Allow to dry.

Clivia

Clivia spp.

Colours: orange/lemon, white

Step 1: To make the pistil, thinly cover a length of fine gauge wire with pale green modelling paste. Allow to dry.

Step 2: Moisten the heads of five stamens and dip in pollen. Tape to the pistil (1).

Step 3: Take a medium-sized ball of modelling paste and hollow out. Make six very shallow cuts around the top (2).

Step 4: Mitre each petal and using a modelling tool, thin the petals by rolling from side to side across the petal. Vein each petal with a cocktail or grooved modelling stick.

Step 5: Push the stamens and pistil into position. Allow to dry before painting.

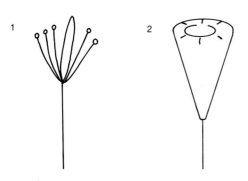

Convolvulus

Convolvulus spp.

Colours: purple, white

Step 1: Tape a bunch of very short stamens to a length of medium gauge wire.

Step 2: Take a medium-sized ball of modelling paste and hollow out to form a cone (1).

Step 3: Make five small cuts around the top edge (2) and gently pull each petal from underneath. Frill each petal and turn backwards (3).

Step 4: Using a modelling tool, gently mark and vein the throat and petals.

Step 5: Insert the stamens and allow to dry before painting.

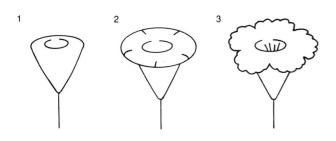

Cornflower

Centaurea spp.

Colours: deep blue

Step 1: Attach a small ball of modelling paste to a length of medium gauge hooked wire. Moisten and cover with blue pollen. Lightly paint the outside edge with eggwhite and dip in yellow pollen. Allow to dry.

Step 2: Take a piece of blue modelling paste and roll out thinly. Using pattern (1), cut three shapes. Using a craft tool, make fine cuts around the edge.

Step 3: Frill the edges using a modelling tool.

Step 4: Moisten the centre of each shape and place one shape on top of the other.

Step 5: Moisten the back of the dry centre and push into the petals.

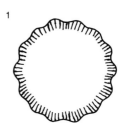

Cosmos

Cosmos spp.

Colours: white, pink, mauve

Step 1: Take a piece of green modelling paste and roll out thinly. Using pattern (1), cut out the calyx. Place in a shallow patty pan to dry.

Step 2: Take a piece of white modelling paste and roll out thinly. Using pattern (2), cut eight petals.

Step 3: Vein, place on foam and bounce gently with a balling tool.

Step 4: Arrange the petals in the moistened calyx, overlapping each one slightly.

Step 5: To make the centre, take a small ball of yellow modelling paste and flatten slightly. Either overpipe with fine dots in royal icing or pattern the top using tulle (3). Paint brown dots around the outer edge and attach to the flower. Allow to dry.

38

Crab-apple

Malus spp.

Colours: pink, red

Pulled method

Step 1: Tape several small-headed stamens to a length of medium gauge wire.

Step 2: Take a small ball of modelling paste and hollow out to form a cone. Make five shallow cuts around the top (1). Gently pull each petal from underneath.

Step 3: Using a modelling tool, frill each petal. Place on foam, and, using a balling tool, bounce each petal.

Step 4: Insert the stamens into the centre and firmly attach.

Step 5: Gently ease and roll the back of the flower down the wire to lengthen.

Step 6: Using scissors, cut a calyx into the lengthened back, pulling the cuts gently outwards. Allow to dry.

Step 7: Paint the calyx green and the back of the flower petals deep pink.

Crocus

Crocus spp.

Colours: various

Step 1: Take a medium-sized ball of lemon modelling paste and hollow out to form a trumpet (1). Insert a length of medium gauge hooked wire. Allow to dry.

Step 2: Take a piece of modelling paste and roll out. Using pattern (2), cut three shapes for the inner petals, leaving the centre of each thick enough to insert a wire. Insert a length of medium gauge wire into each, vein both sides, place on foam and, using a large balling tool, bounce each petal close to the top edge. Allow to dry.

Step 3: Using pattern (3), repeat step 2 for outer petals.

Step 4: Assemble the flower by arranging three small inner petals in position around the trumpet, then arrange the larger outer petals in position around the centre.

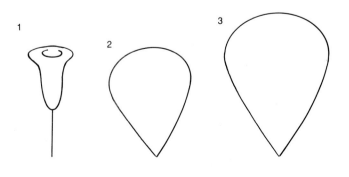

39

Daffodil

Narcissus X

Colours: lemon, white

Step 1: Tape yellow stamens to a length of heavy gauge wire.

Step 2: Take a large ball of lemon modelling paste and hollow out to form a trumpet.

Step 3: Finger and flute the top edge and turn outwards (1).

Step 4: Insert the stamens, place in drying rack and allow to dry.

Step 5: Take a piece of modelling paste and roll out thinly. Using pattern (2), cut two shapes.

Step 6: Finger and thin the edges, vein and pinch to form points.

Step 7: Place together in a stand alternating the petals.

Step 8: Dampen the base of the trumpet and attach to the petals. Allow to dry.

Step 9: When dry, colour around the base of the trumpet with light green colouring. Colour the inside base of the trumpet with green colouring.

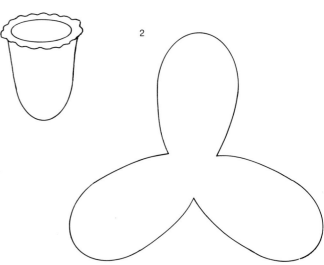

Dahlia

Dahlia X

Colours: various

Step 1: Make the flower centre by winding lemon sewing thread over your fingers until the required thickness. Secure with medium gauge wire through the centre. Cut the threads and trim. Brush with eggwhite and dip in yellow pollen. Allow to dry.

Step 2: Take a piece of green modelling paste and roll out thinly. Using pattern (1), cut out the calyx. Place in a shallow drying stand.

Step 3: Take a piece of modelling paste and roll out thinly. Using pattern (2), cut out eight shapes. Vein and place on foam to bounce gently. Place into the moistened calyx, lightly twisting and overlapping the petals.

Step 4: Moisten the centre of the outer petals and push the dry centre into position.

Step 5: Take a piece of modelling paste and roll out thinly. Using pattern (3), cut five or six inner petals. Shape over a thin modelling tool. Moisten the back of each one and place in position under the centre. Allow to dry.

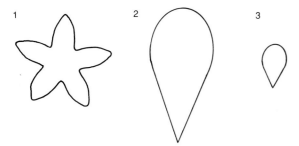

Daisy

Celmisia spp.

Colours: various

Cutter method

Step 1: Take a small ball of yellow modelling paste and attach to a length of medium gauge hooked wire. Allow to dry.

Step 2: Lightly moisten and dip in coloured caster (powdered) sugar. Allow to dry.

Step 3: Take a piece of modelling paste and roll out. Using cutter (1), cut out one piece. Cut each petal in half.

Step 4: Using a small modelling tool, gently press each half petal in the centre to flatten and groove.

Step 5: Moisten the centre of the petals and gently push the sugared centre into place.

Step 6: Arrange the petals. Hang to dry.

41

Daisy, Double

Celmisia spp.

Colours: various

Step 1: Take a small ball of yellow modelling paste and attach to a length of medium gauge hooked wire. Flatten and moisten with eggwhite or gum arabic and dip into coloured gelatine. Allow to dry.

Step 2: Using pattern (1), cut two shapes. Cut each petal in half.

Step 3: Using a modelling tool, gently press each half petal in the centre to flatten and groove (2).

Step 4: Moisten the centre of the petals and attach the second row over the first row. Gently push the dry centre into place.

Step 5: Arrange the petals alternating the second row. Hang to dry.

Daisy, Everlasting

Acroclinium spp.

Colours: various

Step 1: Take a small ball of modelling paste and attach to a length of medium gauge hooked wire. Moisten the top with eggwhite and dip into brown pollen.

Step 2: Lightly paint the outside edge with eggwhite and dip in yellow pollen. Allow to thoroughly dry.

Step 3: Take a piece of modelling paste and roll out thinly. Using pattern (1), cut three shapes. Cut each petal in half.

Step 4: Using a modelling tool, gently press each half petal in the centre to flatten and groove (2).

Step 5: Attach one shape to the dry centre and curve gently around the centre.

Step 6: Attach the two remaining shapes and secure firmly to the centre. Allow to dry.

Step 7: Dust the edges of the petals with powdered chalk or petal dust.

Daisy, Michaelmas

Aster spp.

Colours: blue, white

Step 1: Take a small ball of modelling paste and hollow out.

Step 2: Make many small cuts around the top to form tiny petals (1) and attach to a length of medium gauge wire. Allow to dry.

Step 3: Using yellow royal icing, pipe the centre into the flower. Sprinkle with pollen. Allow to dry.

1

Daphne

Daphne spp.

Colours: pink, white

Step 1: Take a small ball of pink modelling paste and hollow out to form a cone. Insert a length of fine gauge hooked wire.

Step 2: Using scissors, make four evenly spaced cuts around the top edge (1).

Step 3: Mitre the edges of each petal or use the pulled method and gently pull and pinch each petal to a pointed shape (2).

Step 4: Insert the rounded end of a modelling tool into the centre and cup the flower. Allow to dry.

Step 5: Paint the outside of the flower with a deep shade of pink.

1   2

Dianthus

Dianthus spp.

Colours: various

Cutter method

Step 1: Take a small ball of modelling paste and make a small Mexican hat (see page 12).

Step 2: Using cutter (1), cut out the flower shape.

Step 3: Serrate the edges of each petal by making small knicks with a craft tool and gently fluting each petal.

Step 4: Insert a length of fine gauge hooked wire into the centre and then three short fine stamens. Allow to dry.

Step 5: Paint the centres of the petals with the desired colour.

1

Early Nancy

Anguillaria spp.

Colours: pink, white

Step 1: Take a medium-sized ball of modelling paste and make a pixie hat (see page 12).

Step 2: Using cutter (1), cut out the flower.

Step 3: Using scissors, cut deep into the corner of each petal.

Step 4: Place a length of medium gauge hooked wire down the centre.

Step 5: Curve six fine stamens and, using tweezers, put in place evenly around the centre (2).

Step 6: Mould or pipe a small centre. Allow to dry.

Step 7: Colour the edges of the flower as desired.

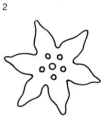

Erica

Erica spp.

Colours: pink

Step 1: Take a small ball of pink modelling paste and push onto a pointed modelling tool to thin.

Step 2: Make six very shallow cuts around the top (1).

Step 3: Mitre each section and thin to form a petal.

Step 4: Reshape on a modelling tool and insert a length of fine gauge wire. Allow to dry.

Step 5: Paint the back of the flower a deeper shade of pink.

Eriostemon

Eriostemon spp.

Colours: white, pink

Cutter method

Step 1: Take a small ball of modelling paste and flatten the top. Hollow out to form a cone.

Step 2: Make five evenly spaced cuts around the top (1).

Step 3: Mitre each petal to shape. Roll with a small balling tool from side to side to thin.

Step 4: Insert a length of fine gauge hooked wire through the centre. Firm at the base and gently curve one or two petals.

Step 5: For the stamens, use only the cotton part, and using tweezers, insert five cottons into the centre of each flower.

Step 6: When dry, paint pink colour on the back of the petals and tip the cotton ends red.

Step 7: To make the bud, take a tiny piece of modelling paste. Wire and when dry tip with deep pink and paint on a tiny green calyx.

Fairy Bells

Colours: various

Cutter method

Step 1: Take a small ball of modelling paste and attach to a length of fine gauge hooked wire. Alternately, use a large headed stamen.

Step 2: Take a piece of modelling paste and roll out thinly. Using cutter (1), cut one piece for the inner petals. Make a hole in the centre and place to dry in an ice ball tray.

Step 3: Take a piece of modelling paste and roll out thinly. Using cutter (2), cut out the outer petals.

Step 4: Thin the edges and, using a pointed modelling tool, gently press each petal in the middle to form a groove.

Step 5: Moisten the centre of the outer petals and place the inner petals of the flower on top.

Step 6: Moisten the centre of the inner petals and insert the dry centre.

Step 7: Gently curl back the outer petals.

Step 8: Hang to dry on a stand.

45

Fantasy Flower

Colours: various

Step 1: Take a piece of modelling paste and roll out thinly. Using pattern (1), cut six petals.

Step 2: Finger and vein each petal then turn over and place on foam. Press your thumb into each petal to shape. Allow to dry.

Step 3: Place a small amount of royal icing on a circle of waxed paper. Arrange three petals for the back row and place a petal in between each back petal for the centre row.

Step 4: Squeeze a small amount of royal icing into the centre and sprinkle with coloured sugar. Allow to dry.

Farewell to Spring

Clarkia spp.

Colours: white with mauve stamens

Step 1: Take a small ball of modelling paste and shape into a cone.

Step 2: Using a craft knife, make a deep cut to divide the top in two. Make two deep cuts across the first cut (1).

Step 3: Using a pointed modelling tool, place in the centre of the flower and gently pull each petal across your index finger to lengthen.

Step 4: Insert five fine mauve stamens.

Note: These flowers may be wired if required by inserting wire up the back.

Five-corners

Styphelia spp.

Colours: pink

Step 1: Tape fine stamen cottons to a'length of fine gauge wire.

Step 2: Take a small ball of cream modelling paste and roll between your fingers to lengthen. Using a modelling tool, hollow out to form a tube (1).

Step 3: Make five evenly spaced cuts around the top and extending approximately one-third down the length of the tube. Mitre each petal to a point, then roll each petal back in a tight roll (2).

Step 4: Insert the wired stamens and firm, making sure the stamens extend well beyond the flower tube (3).

Step 5: Colour with chalk or pale pink alcohol wash and paint on a small green calyx.

Step 6: Form flat pointed leaves (see page 12).

Note: The flowers grow from the base of leaves (4).

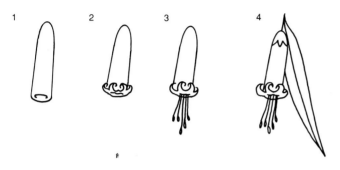

Flannel Flower

Actinotus spp.

Colours: creamy white

Step 1: Take a medium-sized ball of modelling paste and attach to a length of heavy gauge wire. Allow to dry then moisten the top half and dip into a mixture of fine crystal sugar and green chalk (1).

Step 2: Take a piece of modelling paste and roll out thinly. Using pattern (2), cut out approximately ten petals, smooth the edges and vein some.

Note: Flannel flowers are quite uneven and their petals are not always the same size. The number of veined petals varies considerably from flower to flower.

Step 3: Attach to the centre by moistening the base of each petal and firming on. Continue to add petals until the flower is the shape required. Allow to dry.

Step 4: To make the bud, form a centre the same size as the flower centre. Take a medium-sized ball of paste, hollow out and make as many deep cuts as possible around the top and mitre each petal.

Step 5: Pull the centre through and firm.

Step 6: Touch the edges of all petals with chalk or food colouring to match the centre.

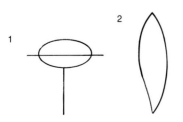

Floppy Flower

Pulled method

Colours: various

Step 1: Take a medium ball of modelling paste and shape into teardrop (1).

Step 2: Flatten the top and, using scissors, make five evenly spaced cuts around the top (2).

Step 3: Pull one side of each cut, then the other side, making heart-shaped petals (3).

Step 4: Push the petals towards the centre, turning the edges back.

Step 5: Insert a grooved modelling tool into the centre to make the throat then push in three to five stamens (4).

Step 6: Place in a drying rack and allow to dry.

Step 7: The throat can be coloured green or yellow. Colour the petals to the desired shade.

  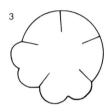 

Flower of the Day

Colours: white, mauve, pink

Step 1: Attach a small ball of modelling paste to a length of medium gauge hooked wire. Brush with eggwhite and dip into coloured pollen. Place five short lemon stamens into the centre at random. Allow to dry.

Step 2: Take a piece of green modelling paste and roll out thinly. Using pattern (1), cut a calyx. Place in a shallow drying stand.

Step 3: Take a piece of modelling paste and roll out thinly. Using pattern (2), cut three petals. Vein and frill the edges.

Step 4: Place in position on the moistened calyx.

Step 5: Moisten the back of the dry flower centre and place in position. Allow to dry.

Step 6: To make the bud, attach a small ball of modelling paste to a length of medium gauge wire. Moisten and dip into coloured pollen. Allow to dry and attach a calyx.

 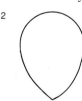

Forget-me-not

Myosotis spp.

Colours: blue, white, pink

Pulled method

Step 1: Take a tiny ball of modelling paste and form into a teardrop. Flatten the top.

48

Step 2: Mark the centre and make five evenly spaced cuts right into the centre.

Step 3: Using the thumb and index finger pull each section from underneath to form petals (1).

Step 4: Insert a yellow stamen into the centre. Allow to dry.

1

Frangipani

Plumeria spp.

Colours: white, pink

Cutter method

Step 1: Take a piece of modelling paste and roll out. Using cutter (1), cut five petals. Keep the petals covered to prevent them drying out.

Step 2: Take one petal and, using a balling tool, thin the edges slightly and curl up the left-hand edge. Repeat with the remaining petals.

Step 3: Moisten the right-hand edge of the first petal and place the second petal onto the first overlapping by about one-third. Continue with all the petals to form a fan shape (2).

Step 4: Quickly roll the flower, overlapping the first and last petals.

Step 5: Firm the base of the flower.

Step 6: Place the flower in a piece of cardboard (3) for support and, with end of a paintbrush, ease the petals out to form the flower size required.

Step 7: Place over an eggcup and allow to dry.

Step 8: Using chalk dust or diluted food colouring, colour the flower centre yellow leaving approximately the top third white.

Step 9: To make the bud, take a medium-sized ball of modelling paste and roll to approximately 2 cm (3/4 inch) long. Form a point at one end. Make five indentations around the bud and gently twist. When completely dry touch with pale yellow colour and paint with diluted burgundy on the indentations.

Note: These flowers can be wired by inserting a length of heavy gauge hooked wire at step 6.

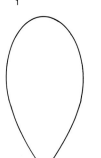

1

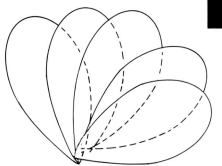

2

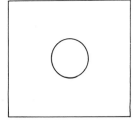

3

Frangipani

Plumeria spp.

Colours: white, pink

Method 2

Step 1: Take a piece of modelling paste and roll out. Using cutter (1), cut five petals. Keep the petals covered to prevent them drying out.

Step 2: Finger the edges of each petal and place over the thumb. Press gently to form a cupped effect.

Step 3: Lift the left-hand side, taking care not to touch the cupped end. Place over a rolling pin to dry. Repeat with the remaining petals. Allow to dry.

Step 4: Pipe a small amount of royal icing onto wax paper in the bottom of an egg carton or eggcup.

Step 5: Arrange the petals in the royal icing making sure each petal is overlapped. Allow to dry thoroughly before removing from the egg carton.

Step 6: Using chalk dust or diluted food colouring, paint the centre yellow, leaving one-third of the petal white.

Step 7: To make the half open flower, take a piece of modelling paste and roll out. Using cutter (1), cut five petals. Keep the petals covered to prevent them drying out.

Step 8: Finger the edges of each petal. Place over the thumb and press gently to form a cupped effect.

Step 9: Lift up both sides of the petal or roll around a modelling tool, making sure not to touch the cupped top edge. Allow to dry flat before painting.

Step 10: Pipe a small amount of royal icing on the base of each petal and overlap the petals in a tight arrangement. Allow to dry.

Note: This flower method cannot be wired.

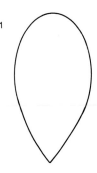

1

Freesia

Freesia spp.

Colours: various

Step 1: Tape three white stamens to a length of medium gauge wire.

Step 2: Take a medium-sized ball of modelling paste and hollow out to form a deep cone (1).

Step 3: Make six evenly spaced shallow cuts around the top. Mitre each section to form petals.

Step 4: Thin each petal and insert a modelling tool into the centre to reshape the bell.

Step 5: Place on foam and using a small balling tool, gently bounce each petal inwards.

Step 6: Insert the wired stamens. Allow to dry.

Step 7: Colour to suit.

Frillies

Colours: various

Cutter method

Step 1: Tape some fine stamens to a length of medium gauge wire.

Step 2: Take a piece of modelling paste and roll out very thinly. Using pattern (1), cut three heart-shaped petals.

Step 3: Frill the edges of the petals and arrange in a shallow drying rack.

Step 4: Insert the stamens and allow to dry.

Step 5: Attach a calyx if required.

Step 6: Colour with chalk, paint or air-brush.

Fuchsia

Fuchsia X

Colours: various

Step 1: Attach a tiny ball of modelling paste to a length of medium gauge wire to make the pistil.

Step 2: Push nine long stamens and one extra long stamen into the paste (1). Allow to dry.

Step 3: Take a piece of modelling paste and roll out thinly. Using pattern (2), cut four petals.

Step 4: Finger the edges and cup the top edge over the thumb.

Step 5: Wrap each petal around the pistil overlapping each one. Allow to dry.

Step 6: Take a piece of modelling paste and roll out thinly. Using pattern (3), cut the sepals.

Step 7: Dampen the centre of the sepals and gently ease the petals into the centre. Firm.

Step 8: Twist the sepal backwards from the petals and allow to dry. Add a small ball of green modelling paste to the base of the sepal.

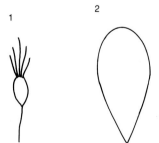

Fuchsia, Double

Fuchsia X

Colours: various

Step 1: Tape several small stamens and one long stamen to a length of medium gauge wire.

Step 2: Take a piece of modelling paste and roll out thinly. Using pattern (1), cut one piece.

Step 3: Frill the edges, pleat, moisten and attach to the stamens. Hang upside down to dry.

Step 4: Take a piece of modelling paste and roll out thinly. Using pattern (1), cut two more pieces. Frill the edges and attach to the dry centre. Hang upside down to dry.

Step 5: Take a piece of modelling paste and roll out thinly. Using pattern (2), cut one or two more pieces. Again frill and attach to the dry centre. Leave to completely dry.

Step 6: Take a piece of modelling paste and roll out thinly. Using pattern (3), cut out the calyx. Vein both sides, moisten and attach to the flower.

Step 7: To complete the flower, add a small ball of modelling paste to the back of the calyx. Allow to dry.

Gardenia

Gardenia spp.

Colours: creamy white

Step 1: Take a large ball of modelling paste and form into a teardrop (1). Attach to a length of heavy gauge wire.

Step 2: Take a piece of modelling paste and roll out thinly. Using pattern (2), cut three or four petals. Moisten and attach to the centre. They should fit tightly around the centre.

Step 3: Take a piece of modelling paste and roll out thinly. Using pattern (3), cut six petals and finger the edges.

Step 4: Arrange the petals overlapping in a drying stand.

Step 5: Moisten the base of the centre and push firmly into position on the overlapping petals. Allow to dry.

Geranium

Geranium spp.

Colours: various

Step 1: Take a small ball of green modelling paste and make a Mexican hat (see page 12). Using pattern (1), cut a calyx. Insert a length of medium gauge wire.

Step 2: Take a piece of modelling paste and roll out thinly. Using pattern (2), cut three petals. Finger the edges and vein lightly.

Step 3: Take a piece of modelling paste and roll out thinly. Using pattern (3), cut two petals.

Step 4: Moisten the back of each petal and arrange in the calyx, placing the three smaller petals to the top and the larger petals at the lower part of the flower.

Step 5: Gently curve the petals backwards.

Step 6: Using a fine modelling tool, make a small hollow in the centre of the flower. Insert stamens to suit the colour of the flower. Allow to dry.

Gladioli

Gladiolus spp.

Step 1: Tape three long stamens and two short stamens to a length of heavy gauge wire.

Step 2: Take a piece of modelling paste and roll out thinly. Using cutter (1), cut six petals.

Step 3: Vein and lightly frill the edges.

Step 4: Moisten the base of three petals and arrange evenly spaced in a deep drying stand.

Step 5: Take the three remaining petals and moisten the base of each. Place side by side, overlapping the base. Roll the first petal inside the third to form a cone.

Step 6: Trim approximately 1.25 cm (1/2 inch) from the base of the cone petals. Moisten the base of the petals in the stand. Place the cone petals in the centre so that they fit between the outer row. Secure well.

Step 7: Moisten the wired stamens and insert into the centre of the flower. Allow to dry.

Step 8: To make the bud, attach a small ball of modelling paste to a length of medium gauge wire. Add a calyx.

Step 9: To make the half open flower, attach a large ball of modelling paste to a length of heavy gauge wire. Using scissors, cut the top in half. Insert a cocktail stick in the cut to thin and form each half into a petal. Fold the two petals into each other and add a calyx.

Godetia

Godetia spp.

Colours: blue, pink, white, lemon

Step 1: Tape ten fine stamens to a length of medium gauge wire.

Step 2: Take a piece of green modelling paste and roll out thinly. Using pattern (1), cut a calyx.

Step 3: Take a piece of white modelling paste and roll out thinly. Using pattern (2), cut four petals.

Step 4: Thin and frill the edges. Attach to the moistened calyx, making sure the petals are overlapping.

Step 5: Insert the stamens. Allow to dry before colouring.

Granny's Bonnets

Colours: various

Step 1: Take a medium-sized ball of modelling paste and make a Mexican hat (see page 12). Using pattern (1), cut one flower.

Step 2: Vein and place on foam and bounce in the centre of the flower.

Step 3: Insert eight to ten long fine stamens into the flower centre. Place in a drying stand.

Step 4: Take a piece of modelling paste and roll out thinly. Using pattern (2), cut three petals.

Step 5: Vein and place on foil in a circle with the points facing outwards.

Step 6: Repeat step 4.

Step 7: Moisten the back of the petals and arrange between each of the rear petals.

Step 8: Moisten the back of the dry centre and push into position. Allow to dry before painting.

Gum Blossom and Gumnut

Eucalyptus spp.

Colours: cream, red, orange, pink

Gum Blossom

Step 1: Wind lemon sewing cotton over the fingers until the required thickness. Secure with a length of medium gauge wire through the centre (1).

Step 2: Cut the cottons and trim.

Step 3: Take a medium-sized ball of green modelling paste and hollow out to form a cup (2).

Step 4: Dampen the centre and place the cottons into position. Allow to dry.

Step 5: Dampen the centre of the cottons and press a very tiny ball of modelling paste into the centre and add a pointed stamen to the centre.

Step 6: Dampen the cotton ends with eggwhite or gum glue and dip in coloured pollen.

Gumnut

Step 1: Take a medium-sized ball of green modelling paste and shape into a teardrop (1).

Step 2: Pull the end of the teardrop to form a stem.

Step 3: Make an indent around the top edge (2).

Step 4: Using a modelling tool, hollow out above the groove. Allow to dry.

Step 5: Paint with brown colouring.

Gypsophila

Gypsophila spp.

Colours: white

Step 1: Tape some very fine stamens or cottons to a length of fine gauge wire. Paint the tips with diluted food colouring.

Step 2: Take a small ball of modelling paste and hollow out to form a cone (1).

Step 3: Insert a veining tool into the centre then pull the stamens through.

Step 4: Make five evenly spaced long cuts around the top and make a small cut between each long one (2).

Step 5: Using the thumb and index finger, gently pull each section from underneath flattening the top slightly as you pull. Allow to dry.

Step 6: Colour the centre with green colouring.

Gypsophila

Gypsophila spp.

Colours: white

Method 2

Step 1: Take a small ball of modelling paste (1) and insert the pointed end of a modelling tool into the centre. Attach to a length of fine gauge hooked wire.

Step 2: Pinch the edge with tweezers (2) and allow to dry.

Step 3: Arrange in a bunch with several buds and flowers.

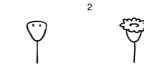

Hibiscus

Hibiscus spp.

Colours: various

Step 1: Tape five large stamens to a long length of heavy gauge wire.

Step 2: Using modelling paste make a long roll approximately 7.5 cm (3 inches) long and thick at the base. Insert the wired stamens down the centre. Bend into a gentle curve. Moisten and dip into lemon pollen effect. Insert stamen cottons around the top and extending down 1.25 cm (1/2 inch).

Step 3: Mark the lower part of the centre by pinching with tweezers (1). Allow to dry.

Step 4: Take a medium-sized ball of green modelling paste and hollow out to make a calyx. Cut around the base to make a second calyx (2). Place into a deep flower stand.

Step 5: Take a piece of modelling paste and roll out thinly. Using pattern (3), cut five petals. Vein and gently flute the edges.

Step 6: Moisten the back of each petal and place in the calyx with the petals overlapping, making sure the last petal is tucked under the first.

Step 7: Secure the dry centre into the flower with eggwhite or runny royal icing. Allow to dry.

Step 8: Take piece of modelling paste and roll out. Using pattern (4), cut another calyx and attach to the base of the flower.

Step 9: To make the bud, take a medium-sized ball of modelling paste and make five shallow cuts around the side. Wire, and, using scissors, cut a double calyx on the base (5). Allow to dry.

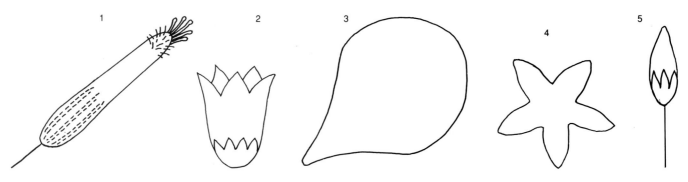

Hippeastrum

Hippeastrum spp.

Colours: various

Cutter method

Step 1: Take a large ball of modelling paste and make a Mexican hat (see page 12). Using pattern (1), cut one flower.

Step 2: Smooth the edges of each petal and vein.

Step 3: Press a large balling tool into the centre to hollow and deepen the centre.

Step 4: Insert one long and three short, large-headed stamens into the centre.

Step 5: Push a length of heavy gauge wire into the back of the flower if required. Allow to dry.

Holly

Ilex spp.

Colours: red, green

Step 1: Take a piece of green modelling paste and roll out thinly. Using pattern (1), cut some leaves. Finger the edges and vein and drape to shape.

Step 2: Take a piece of red modelling paste and form into small balls (2). Allow to dry.

Step 3: Paint the leaves and berries with leaf shine. Allow to dry.

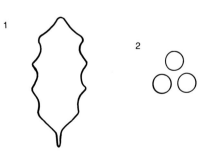

57

Hollyhock, Miniature

Althaea spp.

Colours: various

Cutter method

Step 1: Take a piece of modelling paste and roll out thinly. Using cutter (1), cut several flowers. Keep covered to prevent them drying out.

Step 2: Finger the edges and place on foam. Use a small balling tool to cup each flower.

Step 3: Dampen a large pointed stamen and insert in the centre. Allow to dry.

Step 4: Arrange on a stem with several small buds.

1

Honey Flower

Colours: various

Pulled method

Step 1: Tape some fine stamens to a length of medium gauge wire.

Step 2: Take a medium-sized ball of modelling paste and hollow out to form a cone.

Step 3: Make five evenly spaced shallow cuts around top (1).

Step 4: Gently pull each section to lengthen the petals, then press firmly to flatten.

Step 5: Insert a modelling tool into the cone to reshape the bell.

Step 6: Add the wired stamens and firmly attach the flower to the wire.

Step 7: Twist the petal tops and allow to dry (2).

Step 8: Take a large ball of modelling paste and repeat steps 2–5 for the outer petals.

Step 9: Dampen the back of the dry centre and push it through the middle of the outside petals. Bend the outer petals backwards. Firm and allow to dry.

Step 10: Colour as desired.

1

2

Honeysuckle

Lambertia spp.

Colours: cream

Step 1: Tape together five medium-length and one long stamen on a length of medium gauge wire.

Step 2: Take a small ball of modelling paste and shape into a thin tube approximately 2.5 cm (1 inch) long (1).

Step 3: Hollow out to form a cone and make two long cuts in top. Cut away two sloped pieces leaving a long thin petal (2).

Step 4: Make four shallow cuts into the large section to form the remaining petals. Thin and vein with a modelling tool.

Step 5: Curve the petals and insert the stamens into the centre of the flower (3). Allow to dry.

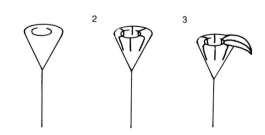

Hyacinth

Hyacinthus spp.

Colours: pastels

Step 1: Take a small ball of modelling paste and hollow out to form a cone shape (1).

Step 2: Make six evenly spaced cuts around the top and approximately half the depth of the cone (2).

Step 3: Mitre each section to form a petal. Using a modelling tool, gently press each petal to soften the edges and thin.

Step 4: Mark a groove down the centre of each petal.

Step 5: Insert a length of fine gauge wire into the centre and turn each petal backwards (3). Allow to dry.

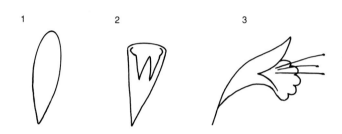

59

Impatiens

Impatiens spp.

Colours: various

Step 1: Attach a tiny ball of modelling paste to a length of medium gauge hooked wire. Make a deep groove in one side (1). Allow to dry.

Step 2: Take a large ball of modelling paste and flatten the top. Make five cuts around the top (2).

Step 3: Pull each petal into shape then thin and gently frill the edge of each one (3).

Step 4: Twist the paste at the back of the flower into a long thin tail. Remove any excess paste if necessary.

Step 5: Push a grooved veining tool into the centre then push the moistened dry centre into position (4). Allow to dry.

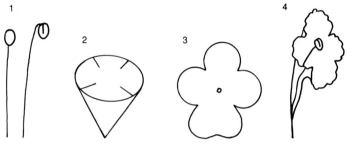

Iris

Iris spp.

Colours: various

Step 1: To make the centre, attach a small ball of modelling paste to a length of medium gauge hooked wire. Hollow out and make three long cuts into the top (1).

Step 2: Gently pull each section to thin and lengthen, then cut a small V out of each (2).

Step 3: Take a large ball of modelling paste and roll out thinly. Using pattern (3), cut three outer petals leaving the centres thick enough to insert wire. Frill the edges and allow to dry in draped position (4).

Step 4: Take a large ball of modelling paste and roll out thinly. Using pattern (5), cut three inner petals. Frill the edges and allow to dry in a curved drying stand.

Step 5: Pipe a heavy yellow line down the centre of the deeply curved outer petals. Allow to dry.

Step 6: Assemble the flower by placing the three inner petals (5) in position around centre then the other petals (3) in alternate positions. Tape the flower tightly together using florist's tape.

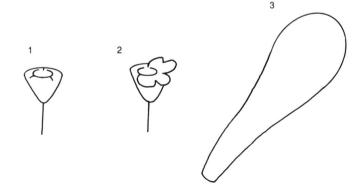

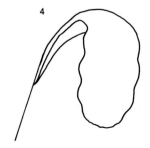

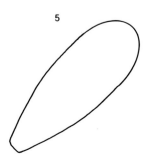

Iris, Wild

Dietus spp.

Colours: white, lemon, mauve

Step 1: Take a small ball of mauve modelling paste and make a Mexican hat (see page 12). Using pattern (1), cut one shape.

Step 2: Cut a small V out of the end of each petal.

Step 3: Turn over and pinch a line down the middle of each petal (2).

Step 4: Holding the thick base, push all three petals towards the middle and into an upright position. Firm and twist the base to remove any excess paste (3). Allow to dry.

Step 5: Take a medium-sized ball of modelling paste and again make a Mexican hat (see page 12). Using pattern (4), cut one shape for the outer petals.

Step 6: Finger and smooth the edges and vein lightly using a corn husk. Place on foam and bounce the back of each petal.

Step 7: Turn over, hollow out the centre and insert a length of medium gauge wire. Gently ease back down the wire and using tweezers, pinch a calyx at the lower edge (5). Allow to dry.

Step 8: Repeat steps 5 and 6. Remove any excess paste from the back. Turn over and gently push into the moistened hollow centre of the outer petals making sure to alternate the petals.

Step 9: Moisten the back of the dry centre and push into position.

Step 10: Paint fine brown dots on the outer petals and shade gently outwards with lemon chalk or petal dust.

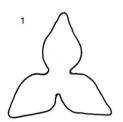
1

2

3

4

5

Irresistibles

Colours: various

Step 1: Take a piece of modelling paste and roll out thinly. Using pattern (1), cut out the centre.

Step 2: Moisten the head of a large pointed stamen and insert into the centre. Allow to dry before painting.

Step 3: Take a piece of modelling paste and roll out thinly. Using pattern (2), cut the flower back. Place on foam and gently bounce each petal.

Step 4: Turn over, moisten the centre and push the dry flower centre into position. Allow to dry before painting.

1

2

61

Jacaranda

Jacaranda spp.

Colours: mauve

Step 1: Take a large ball of modelling paste and hollow out to form a long trumpet.

Step 2: Allow one-third for the base petal and, using scissors, divide the remaining two-thirds into four equal sections (1).

Step 3: Gently pull out the petals. Frill all the edges and then reshape the hollow centre.

Step 4: Insert a length of medium gauge hooked wire and one round-headed stamen.

Step 5: Gently flatten the tube section of the flower (2).

Jasmine

Jasminum spp.

Colours: pink, white

Cutter method

Step 1: Take a small ball of modelling paste and flatten the top. Hollow out with a small modelling tool to make a fine cone

Step 2: Using scissors, make five evenly spaced cuts well down into the cone (1).

Step 3: Cut the sharp corners off each petal to give a rounded edge (2). Finger gently to neaten the edges or use a cocktail stick and roll side to side.

Step 4: Insert a length of fine gauge wire into the centre easing the paste gently down the wire to form a fine thin back to the flower.

Step 5: Add one fine white, pale green or lemon stamen into the centre of the flower. Allow it to show just above the flower centre. Allow to dry.

Step 6: Paint with pale pink alcohol wash. Paint a tiny calyx in a brownish-green.

Step 7: To make the buds, insert a length of fine gauge wire into a tiny ball of modelling paste. Roll between the thumb and index finger just below the top, thinning the bud down the wire to taper (3). Allow to dry.

Step 8: Paint a deeper pink than the flower shading down to brownish green to form a calyx.

Jasmine

Jasminum spp.

Colours: pink, white

Pulled method

Step 1: Take a small ball of modelling paste and flatten the top. Hollow out with a fine modelling tool to make a cone (1).

Step 2: Using scissors, make five evenly spaced cuts in the rim (2).

Step 3: Using the thumb and index finger gently pull the petals to lengthen (3).

Step 4: Insert a pale green, lemon or white stamen into the centre allowing it to protrude just above the flower centre. Allow to dry.

Step 5: Paint the back of flower with pale pink alcohol wash. Paint a tiny calyx in brownish-green.

Step 6: Make the bud the same as the Cutter method above (4).

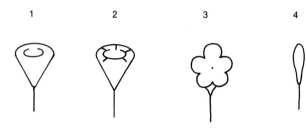

Jonquil

Narcissus spp.

Colours: white, lemon

Step 1: Take a medium-sized ball of modelling paste and make a Mexican hat (see page 12). Using pattern (3), cut out a calyx.

Step 2: Hook a length of medium gauge wire into the centre.

Step 3: Twist the excess paste from the calyx down the wire to form a long back.

Step 4: Take a small ball of yellow modelling paste and hollow out to form a cup (1). Allow to dry.

Step 5: Take a piece of pale cream modelling paste and roll out thinly. Using pattern (2), cut two pieces.

Step 6: Finger and vein the petals and place the second shape inside the first, alternating the petals.

Step 7: Dampen the base of the centre and attach to the petals.

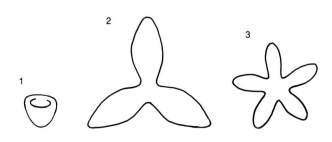

Lasiandra osbeckia

Tibouchina spp.

Colours: purple, pink

Step 1: To make the pistil, cover a length of fine gauge wire with green modelling paste. Curve gently and tape together with several curved stamens (1).

Step 2: Take a piece of green modelling paste and roll out thinly. Using pattern (2), cut out a calyx and place in the centre of a large flower ring.

Step 3: Take a piece of modelling paste and roll out thinly. Using pattern (3), cut five petals. Vein and gently flute the edge of each one. Place in position on the moistened calyx.

Step 4: Push the stamens into position. Allow to dry.

Step 5: When the flower is dry, complete the calyx by adding a medium-sized cone-shaped piece of green modelling paste (4). Thread it onto the wire and attach to the moistened back of the calyx.

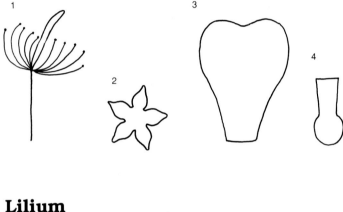

Lilium

Lilium X

Colours: various

Step 1: Tape one long large-headed stamen and six shorter stamens to a length of heavy gauge wire.

Step 2: Take a piece of modelling paste and roll out. Using pattern (1), cut a calyx. Place in a deep drying stand.

Step 3: Take a piece of modelling paste and roll out thinly. Using pattern (2), cut two pieces. Finger the edges and vein the petals and arrange on the calyx, making sure to alternate the petals.

Step 4: Insert the stamens and allow to dry.

Step 5: Moisten a small ball of green modelling paste and add to base of the calyx. Allow to dry.

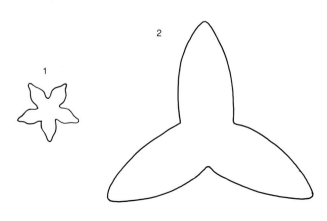

64

Lily, Arum

Zantedeschia spp.

Colours: white

Step 1: Hook a length of medium gauge wire.

Step 2: Mould a long piece of yellow modelling paste onto the hooked wire to make a spadix (1). Allow to dry.

Step 3: Using a slightly damp brush dampen the spadix and coat with a mixture of yellow chalk and caster (powdered) sugar. Allow to dry.

Step 4: Take a piece of white modelling paste and roll out thinly. Using pattern (2), cut one flower.

Step 5: Smooth and thin the edges then lightly vein and shade the lower edge pale green.

Step 6: Moisten the lower edge and wrap around the dry spadix slightly twisting one side over the other (3). Allow to dry.

Step 7: Add a deeper shade of green on the outside base.

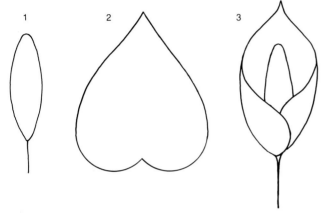

Lily, Brazilian

Mandevilla spp.

Colours: various

Cutter method

Step 1: Take a large ball of modelling paste and make a Mexican hat (see page 12).

Step 2: Using cutter (1), cut one flower.

Step 3: Finger the sides and vein slightly. Frill the rounded side of the petals.

Step 4: Insert a modelling tool into the centre of the flower and hollow out slightly to form a tube.

Step 5: Insert a length of heavy gauge wire and then the stamens. Allow to dry completely before painting.

Lily, Day

Hemerocallis spp.

Colours: various

Cutter method

Step 1: Take a medium-sized ball of modelling paste and make a Mexican hat (see page 12).

Step 2: Using cutter (1), cut one flower.

Step 3: Finger the edges, vein and gently pinch the centre of each petal.

Step 4: Insert a modelling tool into the centre and hollow out slightly to form a tube.

Step 5: Tape stamens onto a length of heavy gauge wire. Insert in the flower.

Step 6: Arrange the petals and allow to completely dry before colouring.

Lily, Eucharist

Eucharis spp.

Colours: white/green

Step 1: Take a large ball of modelling paste and use a modelling tool to hollow out about half the depth (1).

Step 2: Cut six peaks round the edge. Then cut two lower points (2) between these peaks.

Step 3: Cut short pieces of stamen cottons and attach to the long peaks with a little eggwhite.

Step 4: Push one long stamen into the centre of the throat. Allow to dry.

Step 5: Take a piece of modelling paste and roll out thinly. Using pattern (3), cut six petals. Vein and gently flute the edges with a modelling tool.

Step 6: Moisten the back and place in position (4) over a flower ring.

Step 7: Moisten the back of the dry centre and place in position. Allow to dry.

Note: If you need to wire the flower, add a wired calyx.

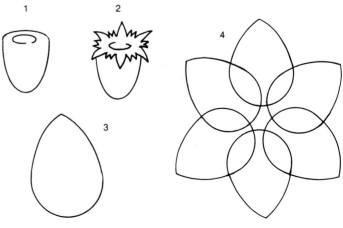

Lily, Tiger

Lilium spp.

Colours: various

Step 1: Take a piece of modelling paste and roll out thinly. Using pattern (1), cut six petals leaving the centres thick enough to take wire.

Step 2: Finger the edges, vein and allow to dry in a curved drying stand.

Step 3: Take six heavy long stamens and mould small pieces of modelling paste on the end of each to form the anthus.

Step 4: Make the stigma by attaching a small ball of modelling paste to a length of medium gauge wire. When dry tape the stigma and stamens together.

Step 5: Place the petals evenly around the centre and tape together with florist's tape.

Step 6: Paint or pipe spots on the petals.

Alternate method:

Step 1: Take a piece of modelling paste and roll out thinly. Using pattern (1), cut six petals.

Step 2: Finger edges, vein and allow to dry in a curved drying stand.

Step 3: Take six heavy long stamens and mould small pieces of modelling paste on the end of each to form the anthus.

Step 4: Make the stigma by attaching a small ball of modelling paste to a heavy stamen. Allow to dry.

Step 5: Place a small amount of firm royal icing into a deep drying stand and arrange three petals in position. Arrange the next three petals in alternate positions.

Step 6: Place the stigma and anthus in position. Allow to dry.

Step 7: Paint or pipe spots on the petals.

Lily of the Valley

Convellaria spp.

Colours: white, pink

Cutter method

Step 1: Take a piece of modelling paste and roll out thinly. Using cutter (1), cut seven to ten flowers. Keep covered to prevent them drying out.

Step 2: Push one flower over the end of small balled modelling tool. Work until the edges are fine, but keep the thickness in the centre.

Step 3: Moisten the head of a fine stamen or knotted wire and insert into the flower. Allow to dry.

Step 4: Tape several small buds and seven to ten flower heads along a stem.

Alternate method:

Step 1: Take a small ball of modelling paste and hollow out to form a small cup. Insert a length of fine gauge hooked wire into the centre and serrate the edge of the cup by pinching with tweezers. Allow to dry.

Step 2: Thread a tiny ball of green onto the wire and attach to the back of the flower. Allow to dry.

Lisianthus

Lisianthus spp.

Colours: various

Step 1: Attach a tiny ball of modelling paste to a length of medium gauge wire. Moisten and dip the ball into green pollen to form a pistil.

Step 2: Take five pointed stamens, moisten and dip into yellow pollen. Allow to dry, then tape the stamens around the ball.

Step 3: Take a piece of modelling paste and roll out thinly. Using pattern (1), cut out a calyx and place in a deep drying stand.

Step 4: Take a piece of modelling paste and roll out thinly. Using pattern (2), cut five petals. Finger the edges and vein. Moisten the back of each and place in a clockwise position on the calyx. Overlap each petal and tuck the last petal under the first.

Step 5: Push the centre stamens into position and allow to dry.

Step 6: Paint or chalk the petals around the base of the stamen.

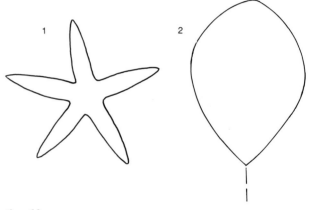

Lobelia

Lobelia spp.

Colours: purple

Pulled method

Step 1: Take a small ball of modelling paste and hollow out to form a cone. Insert a length of fine gauge wire and make cuts into the top (1).

Step 2: Pull and thin each petal and, using a modelling tool, gently flute the lower petals.

Step 3: Using a pointed modelling tool, mark a vein down the centre of each lower side petal.

Step 4: Twist the top petals towards the outside (2). Allow to dry before painting making sure to leave the centre section white.

Lotus

Nymphaea spp.

Colours: various

Step 1: Tape three pointed-head stamens to a length of medium gauge wire.

68

Step 2: Take a piece of modelling paste and roll out thinly. Using patterns (1, 2, 3 and 4), cut one shape from each.

Step 3: Place each one on foam and, using a balling tool, gently pull each petal towards the centre.

Step 4: Place shape (1) into a drying stand. Moisten the centre and place (2) into position. Repeat with shapes (3) and (4).

Step 5: Pull the stamens into position through the centre of the flower. Allow to dry before colouring.

Magnolia

Magnolia spp.

Colours: cream with mauve

Step 1: Attach a large ball of modelling paste to a length of heavy gauge wire. Form into a flower centre (1).

Step 2: Insert stamen cottons thickly around the top of the centre (2). Mark a small dent on the top. Allow to dry.

Step 3: Take a piece of modelling paste and roll out. Using pattern (3), cut three inner petals leaving the centres thick enough to take wire. Insert a length of heavy gauge wire into each petal. Vein and dry in a curved drying stand.

Step 4: Take a piece of modelling paste and roll out. Using pattern (4), cut three outer petals leaving the centres thick enough to take wire. Insert a length of heavy gauge wire into each petal. Vein and dry in a curved drying stand.

Step 5: Colour the back of the petals then assemble around the centre using petals (4) then (3).

Step 6: To make the bud, mould a large ball of modelling paste onto a length of heavy gauge wire. Moisten and dip into powdered gelatine.

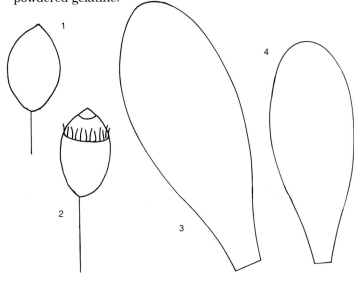

69

Maidenhair Fern

Adiantum spp.

Colours: green

Step 1: Push a small ball of green modelling paste onto a length of medium gauge green wire. Push it halfway down. Flatten onto the wire and, using fine scissors, cut knicks into the top (1).

Step 2: Repeat step 1 three times, moving up the same wire each time.

Step 3: Cover the end of the wire with a tiny ball of modelling paste. Flatten and cut knicks into the top. Allow to dry.

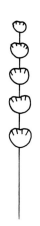

Meadow Bells

Colours: various

Flowers

Step 1: Take a medium-sized ball of modelling paste and hollow out into a long trumpet.

Step 2: Make six evenly spaced shallow cuts around the top (1).

Step 3: Pull each section from underneath to make an oval-shaped petal.

Step 4: Push a hooked wire through the centre of the flower. Allow to dry.

Step 5: Paint the centre yellow and paint the petal tops with leaf shine to give a waxed finish.

Leaves

Step 1: Take a piece of modelling paste and roll out thinly. Using pattern (2) cut out a leaf. Finger edges and vein. Allow to dry.

Step 2: Paint dark green then coat with leaf shine to give a gloss.

Mist Flower

Colours: various

Cutter method

Step 1: Tape some fine stamens to a length of medium gauge wire.

Step 2: Take a piece of modelling paste and roll out very thinly. Using cutter (1), cut the flower centre.

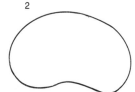

Step 3: Finger the edges, place on foam and, using a balling tool, make a cup.

Step 4: Take a medium-sized ball of modelling paste and make a witch's hat (see page 12). Using pattern (2), cut a flower back.

Step 5: Finger and pinch the edges of each petal, twisting lightly.

Step 6: Dampen the centre and place the cupped piece in position.

Step 7: Push the wired stamens through the flower. Allow to dry in a drying stand.

Step 8: Colour as required.

Oleander

Nerium spp.

Colours: various

Step 1: Attach a tiny ball of modelling paste to a length of heavy gauge hooked wire. Roll as shown (1) to form a pistil. Allow to dry then moisten and dip in yellow pollen.

Step 2: Take a large ball of modelling paste and make a Mexican hat (see page 12). Using pattern (2), cut one piece for the outer petals.

Step 3: Frill each petal and gently ease a balling tool into the throat.

Step 4: Take a piece of modelling paste and roll out thinly. Using pattern (3), cut one piece for the inner petals.

Step 5: Cut into the edges of the inner petals as shown (4). Paint pink strips down the cuts while still wet.

Step 6: Moisten the throat of the flower and place the inner petals in position.

Step 7: Insert the pistil. Allow to dry before painting.

Orange Blossom

Citrus sinensis

Colours: cream

Step 1: Take a piece of modelling paste and roll out thinly. Cut a strip approximately 1.25 cm (1/2 inch) wide and 2.5 cm (1 inch) long. Using scissors, cut into a very fine fringe (1).

Step 2: Roll the fringe around five stamens to form the centre (2). Insert a length of medium gauge wire and allow to dry.

Step 3: Take a piece of modelling paste and roll out thinly. Using pattern (3), cut the petals. Thin the edges and slightly curve each petal backwards.

Step 4: Moisten the centre and place the stamens in position. Allow to dry.

Alternate method:

Step 1: Take a piece of modelling paste and roll out thinly. Cut a strip approximately 1.25 cm (1/2 inch) wide and 2.5 cm (1 inch) long. Using scissors, cut into a very fine fringe (1).

Step 2: Roll the fringe around five stamens to form the centre (4). Allow to dry.

Step 3: Take a piece of modelling paste and roll out thinly. Using pattern (5), cut five petals. Finger the edges and attach to the dry centre. Allow to dry.

Step 4: Add a calyx.

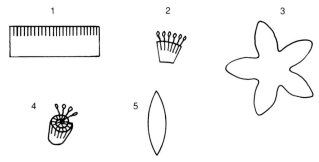

Orange Blossom, Mexican

Choisya spp.

Colours: various

Pulled method

Step 1: Tape stamens to a length of medium gauge wire.

Step 2: Take a medium-sized ball of modelling paste, flatten the top and hollow out the centre.

Step 3: Make five evenly spaced cuts around the top (1). Push the stamens through the centre and secure. Using the thumb and index finger, pull each section from underneath (2). Allow to dry. Colour to suit.

Step 4: To make a bud, hook a wire and push into a medium-sized ball of modelling paste. Secure firmly. Make five indents around the top with the back of a knife and paint a green calyx (3).

Orange Blossom, Mock

Philadelphus spp.

Colours: white/cream

Step 1: Take a piece of modelling paste and either finger out or roll out thinly. Using pattern (1), cut four petals.

Step 2: Place on foam and push gently in the centre with the thumb to cup up. Allow to dry.

Step 3: Take a piece of modelling paste and roll out thinly. Using pattern (2), cut a calyx. Finger out to thin the edges.

Step 4: Add a small amount of royal icing to the calyx centre and arrange the dry petals.

Step 5: Completely cover the centre with fine stamens.

Orchid, Bauhinia Tree

Bauhinia spp.

Colours: various

Step 1: To make the seed pod/pistil, cover a piece of fine gauge wire with a small amount of modelling paste. Curve gently and add a stamen head to the tip. Allow to dry.

Step 2: Tape five long stamens to the seed pod/pistil, using florist's tape, to form the centre.

Step 3: Take a piece of modelling paste and roll out. Using pattern (1), cut one top petal, leaving the centre thick enough to insert a length of medium gauge wire. Vein and gently flute the edges. Allow to dry in a curved stand or cornflour (cornstarch) box.

Step 4: Take a piece of modelling paste and roll out. Using pattern (2), cut two wing petals. Make sure to reverse the pattern to make a pair. Leave the centres thick enough to insert wire. Vein and gently flute the edges and allow to dry in a curved drying stand.

Step 5: Take a piece of modelling paste and roll out. Using pattern (3), cut two lower petals and repeat as for step 4. Allow to dry.

Step 6: Colour the petals and tape the centre and petals together (4).

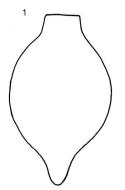
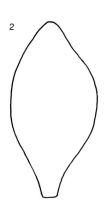
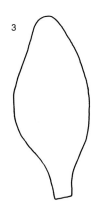
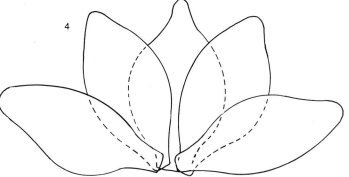

Orchid, Bush

Colours: various

Pulled method

Step 1: Take a medium-sized ball of modelling paste and hollow out.

Step 2: Make five cuts around the top as shown (1).

Step 3: Pinch and pull out the top four petals.

Step 4: Flatten and gently pull the large petal from underneath. This will form the tongue.

Step 5: Vein each petal using a cocktail stick.

Step 6: Arrange the petals then insert a length of medium gauge hooked wire.

Step 7: Insert some medium-length stamens into the centre of the flower. Allow to dry before painting fine dots on the tongue.

Step 8: To make the bud, take a small ball of modelling paste and attach to a length of medium gauge wire.

Step 9: Using scissors, cut the top in half and then in quarters (2).

Step 10: Press and thin each petal with a modelling tool. Arrange the petals and allow to dry. Colour as desired.

Orchid, Cattleya

Cattleya spp.

Colours: various

Step 1: Take a piece of modelling paste and roll out. Using pattern (1), cut one piece for the throat leaving the centre thick enough to insert wire. Vein and heavily frill the edges. Shape around a modelling tool and allow to dry in a cornflour (cornstarch) box.

Step 2: Take a piece of modelling paste and roll out. Using pattern (2), cut three sepals. Vein and thin the edges and place in position in a shallow curved drying stand.

Step 3: Take a piece of modelling paste and roll out. Using pattern (3), cut two petals. Frill the edges and vein. Moisten the back of each petal and place in position.

Step 4: Moisten the back of the dry throat and push into the centre of the orchid. Allow to dry thoroughly.

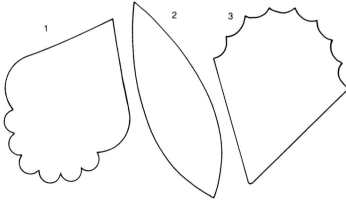

74

Orchid, Cooktown

Dendrobium spp.

Colours: magenta

Step 1: Shape a small ball of modelling paste onto a length of medium gauge wire to form the column. Using a small modelling tool, groove the underside and cup over (1). Allow to dry.

Step 2: Take a piece of modelling paste and roll out thinly. Using pattern (2), cut one throat. Vein with a cornhusk. Dampen the throat and wrap around the dry column. Allow to dry by draping gently over cotton wool or in a cornflour (cornstarch) box.

Step 3: Take a piece of modelling paste and roll out thinly. Using pattern (3), cut one piece for the sepals. Finger the edges and vein.

Step 4: Take a piece of modelling paste and roll out thinly. Using pattern (4), cut two petals. Finger the edges, vein and gently curve.

Step 5: Place the sepals in position. Moisten and attach the petals, one to either side and push the dry column and throat pieces into the soft petals. Allow to dry flat.

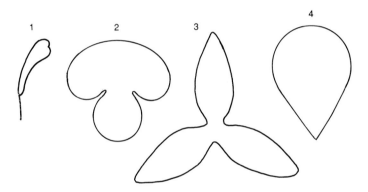

Orchid, Crucifix

Epidendrum spp.

Colours: orange, red

Step 1: Take a piece of modelling paste and roll out, not too thinly. Using pattern (1), cut the throat.

Step 2: Thin and gently frill the edges and mark two lines down the centre, using tweezers. Insert a stamen in the thick end of the throat. Allow to dry.

Step 3: Take a piece of modelling paste and roll out thinly. Using pattern (2), cut the rear petals.

Step 4: Finger the edges and, using a modelling tool, vein down the centre of each petal.

Step 5: Moisten the centre and attach to the throat. Allow to dry.

Orchid, Cymbidium

Cymbidium X

Colours: various

Easy method

Step 1: Take a piece of modelling paste and roll out thinly. Using pattern (1), cut one piece for the throat. Finger the edges and frill the centre section. Shape around a modelling tool. Allow to dry in a cornflour (constarch) box.

Step 2: Make the column by rolling a piece of modelling paste in your fingers. Using a small balling tool, groove the underside and curve gently (2).

Step 3: Moisten and attach to the dry throat. Allow to dry.

Step 4: Take a piece of modelling paste and roll out. Using pattern (3), cut two petals and three sepals. Finger the edges and vein.

Step 5: Arrange the sepals in a shallow pan.

Step 6: Moisten and attach the petals.

Step 7: Dampen the centre and push the dry throat and column into the wet petals. Support with cotton wool until dry.

Step 8: Colour as desired.

Step 9: Pipe two yellow lines along the throat centre.

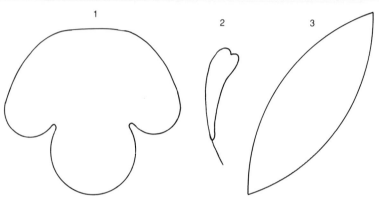

Orchid, Cymbidium

Cymbidium X

Colours: various

Wired method

Step 1: Shape a small ball of modelling paste onto a length of medium gauge wire. Using a small balling tool, groove the underside and curve gently for the column (1). Allow to dry.

Step 2: Take a small ball of modelling paste and insert a length of moistened medium gauge wire. Roll out, leaving the paste a little thicker in the centre over the wire. Using pattern (2), cut one piece for the throat. Finger the edges and frill the centre section. Arrange the lobes upwards and dry in a curved drying stand or cornflour (cornstarch) box.

Step 3: Take a piece of modelling paste and insert a length of medium gauge wire. Roll out, leaving the paste a little thicker in the centre over the wire. Using pattern (3), cut two petals and three sepals (4). Finger the edges and vein. Allow to dry in a curved shape.

Step 4: Place the column in the tongue, position the petals and sepals and tape securely together with florist's tape.

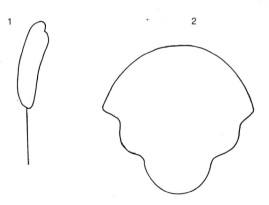

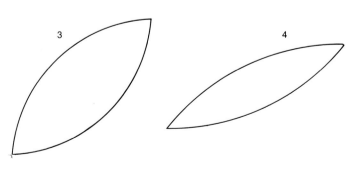

76

Orchid, Java

Dendrobium spp.

Colours: various

Step 1: Make a very small bud on a length of heavy gauge hooked wire (1). Allow to dry.

Step 2: Take a piece of modelling paste and roll out thinly. Using pattern (2), cut one throat.

Step 3: Make a small slit on either side to form wings. Frill the centre section.

Step 4: Wrap around the bud completely, using a little water to attach. Allow to dry.

Step 5: Take a piece of modelling paste and roll out thinly. Using pattern (3), cut one piece.

Step 6: Thin the edges and extend the wing petals by rolling slightly.

Step 7: Using a balling tool, cup the wing petals on a piece of foam then turn over.

Step 8: Using a balling tool, pull the other three petals towards the centre.

Step 9: Make a hole in the centre and place in a patty pan to dry.

Step 10: Attach the throat section to back of the flower with a small amount of royal icing.

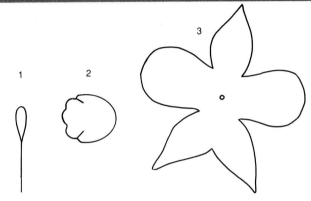

Orchid, Lady's Slipper

Paphiopedilum spp.

Colours: various

Step 1: Take a small ball of modelling paste and attach to a length of heavy gauge hooked wire for the staminode (1). Allow to dry.

Step 2: Insert a length of moistened medium gauge wire into a ball of modelling paste and roll out leaving paste a little thicker in the centre over the wire. Using pattern (2), cut the dorsal sepal. Thin and frill the edges and bounce on foam to gently curve.

Step 3: Take a piece of modelling paste and insert a length of medium gauge wire. Using pattern (3), cut two petals. Thin and frill the edges and place on foam to gently curve.

Step 4: Take a medium-sized ball of modelling paste and hollow out using a balling tool. Pull the top edge backwards, finger and thin this edge. Pinch a lip in the front and cut a small V shape from the back (4). Insert a balling tool to reform the centre.

Step 5: Attach the staminode to the V section of the column with eggwhite or gum glue. Allow all pieces to completely dry.

Step 6: Paint all pieces and assemble by taping together.

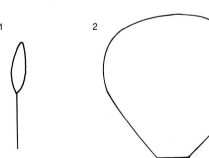

Orchid, Laelia

Laelia spp.

Colours: various

Cutter and pulled method

Step 1: Take a small ball of modelling paste and form a teardrop (1).

Step 2: Flatten the thick end to make the lip of the orchid (2).

Step 3: Using a modelling tool, frill this edge.

Step 4: Insert a modelling tool into the thick section and hollow out.

Step 5: Pull the top section forward and use tweezers to mark two grooves in the throat.

Step 6: Insert a length of medium gauge wire and allow to dry.

Step 7: Take a piece of modelling paste and roll out thinly. Using pattern (3), cut one piece. Finger the edges and lightly vein each petal.

Step 8: Gently ease the two lower petals apart.

Step 9: Moisten the centre and push the throat into position and turn the dorsal sepal forward. Allow to dry.

Orchid, Lycaste

Lycaste spp.

Colours: pink, white, lemon

Step 1: Take a medium-sized ball of modelling paste and attach to a length of medium gauge hooked wire.

Step 2: Hollow out the top portion to form a cone. Bring one side to a point, tipping gently forward (1). Allow to dry.

Step 3: Take a piece of modelling paste and roll out thinly. Using pattern (2), cut three petals. Finger each petal to remove the cut edge.

Step 4: Frill the front petal and attach the three to the centre. Allow to dry.

Step 5: Take a ball of modelling paste and roll out thinly. Using pattern (3), cut the outer petals. Finger the cut edges and vein.

Step 6: Attach to the centre and allow to completely dry before painting.

  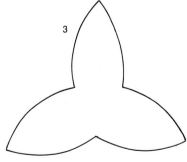

Orchid, Mini

Colours: various

Cutter method

Step 1: Take a tiny ball of modelling paste and form a column on a length of medium gauge hooked wire (1). Allow to dry.

Step 2: Take a piece of modelling paste and roll out thinly. Using cutter (2), cut one throat. Finger the edges and attach to the column. Allow to dry.

Step 3: Take a piece of modelling paste and roll out thinly. Using cutter (3), cut the orchid back.

Step 4: Thin the edges, place on foam and, using a balling tool, gently curve the petals.

Step 5: Moisten the centre and push the wired throat through. Allow to dry and colour as desired.

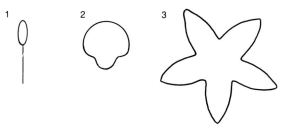

Orchid, Phalaenopsis

Phalaenopsis spp.

Colours: white, pink/mauve

Step 1: Place a small ball of modelling paste on a length of heavy gauge wire. Mark the centre with a groove to form a column (1). Brush with eggwhite and cover with yellow pollen. Allow to dry.

Step 2: Take a piece of modelling paste and roll out thinly. Using pattern (2), cut one throat. Finger the edges and cut as marked.

Step 3: Using a large balling tool, bounce the lobes of the throat on a piece of foam. Using a medium balling tool, pull towards the centre and curve gently. Pierce a hole in the centre. Leave to dry in the bottom of a patty pan before painting.

Step 4: Take a piece of modelling paste and roll out thinly. Using pattern (3), cut the back sepals. Finger, vein and place in a shallow curved drying stand.

Step 5: Take a piece of modelling paste and roll out thinly. Using pattern (4), cut two wing petals, making sure to reverse the pattern for one of them. Finger and vein and moisten the back. Place in position on the back sepals.

Step 6: Moisten the back of the throat and place in the centre of the petals.

Step 7: Moisten the column and push carefully through the throat and petals. Allow to dry.

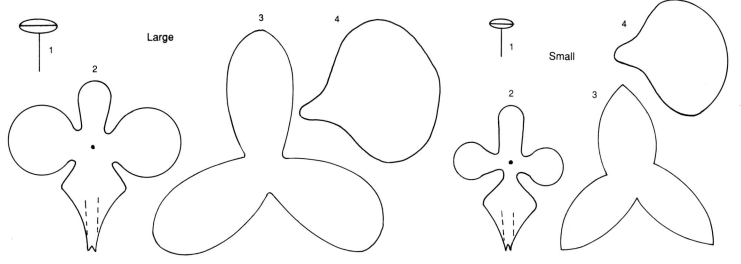

Orchid, Rock

Colours: various

Step 1: Dip a stamen head into runny royal icing (1). Allow to dry.

Step 2: Take a piece of modelling paste and roll out thinly. Using pattern (2), cut a small circle to form the throat. Moisten and attach to the centre. Allow to dry.

Step 3: Using pattern (3), cut one piece.

Step 4: Dampen the back of the throat and push into position with one petal at the top.

Step 5: Curl the two side petals back and the top petal forward. Allow to dry and colour as required.

Orchid, Royal Bifrenaria

Bifrenaria spp.

Colours: various

Step 1: Take a piece of modelling paste and make a column. Attach to a length of medium gauge wire (1). Allow to dry.

Step 2: Take a piece of modelling paste and roll out thinly. Using pattern (2), cut a throat. Vein and frill, moisten and attach to the column. Allow to dry.

Step 3: Take a piece of modelling paste and roll out thinly. Using pattern (3), cut five petals. Smooth the edges, vein and bounce three petals. Vein and frill the edges of the remaining two petals.

Step 4: Overlap and join all the petals in a half circle (4).

Step 5: Moisten the back of the throat and wrap the petals around. Dry in a deep drying stand.

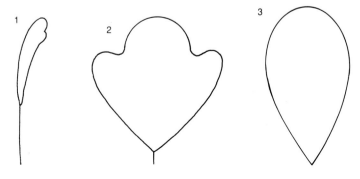

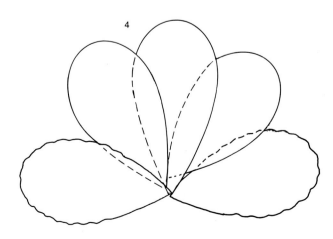

Orchid, Singapore

Dendrobium spp.

Colours: various

Step 1: Make the column by shaping a small ball of modelling paste on to a length of medium gauge wire (1). Gently ball out underneath and allow to dry before dusting with yellow chalk.

Step 2: Take a piece of modelling paste and roll out thinly. Using pattern (2), cut the throat. Gently vein with a corn husk and frill the centre section. Dampen the column and wrap the throat around the column. Allow to dry.

Step 3: Take a piece of modelling paste and roll into a log shape. Insert a length of medium gauge wire. Roll out the paste taking care to keep the wire in the centre. Using pattern (3) cut one sepal. Repeat this step to make another two sepals.

Step 4: Using pattern (4), cut one petal. Repeat this step to make another petal, making sure to reverse the pattern. Vein with a corn husk and drape to dry.

Step 5: Colour all sepals and the petals by brushing with yellow chalk at the base.

Step 6: Take the dorsal sepal (3) then place a petal (4) on each side and to the front of the centre sepal. Put two lower sepals in position before placing the column and throat in the centre.

Step 7: Tape securely with florist's tape.

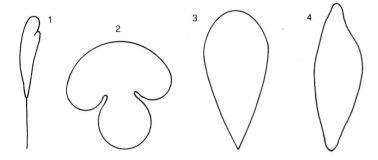

Orchid, Singapore

Dendrobium spp.

Colours: various

Quick cutter method

Step 1: Shape a very small bud on a length of heavy gauge hooked wire for the column (1). Allow to dry.

Step 2: Take a ball of modelling paste and roll out thinly. Using pattern (2), cut one throat.

Step 3: Make a small slit on either side to form wings. Frill the centre section.

Step 4: Attach to the bud by dampening and wrapping completely around. Allow to dry.

Step 5: Take a piece of modelling paste and roll out thinly. Using pattern (3), cut one piece.

Step 6: Finger the edges to neaten.

Step 7: Using a balling tool, pull all petals towards the centre.

Step 8: Make a hole in the centre and place in a patty pan. Allow to dry.

Step 9: Attach the throat section to the back of the flower with a small amount of royal icing.

Step 10: Colour to suit.

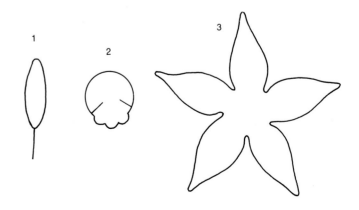

Orchid, Sun

Thelymitra orchidaceae

Colours: mauve

Step 1: Make the throat by placing a small ball of modelling paste onto a length of medium gauge wire.

Step 2: Using scissors, cut the top in half then one side in half again (1). Flatten the two small sections (2). Allow to dry.

Step 3: Using pattern (3), cut two pieces. Finger the edges and vein.

Step 4: Place in a shallow drying stand, making sure the petals alternate.

Step 5: Moisten the back of the throat with eggwhite and insert into the layered petals. Allow to dry before adding the spots.

Orchid, Tropical Jewel

Colours: various

Cutter method

Step 1: Take a piece of modelling paste and roll out thinly. Using cutter (1), cut one throat. Frill the edges and wrap around a modelling tool to curve. Place in cornflour (corn-starch) box to dry.

Step 2: Take a small ball of modelling paste and form a long teardrop for the column. Pull the top edge to the left then right (2). Mould around a point brush handle to produce a deep groove on the underside. Attach to the inside of the throat with water or gum glue. Allow to dry.

Step 3: Take a piece of modelling paste and roll out thinly. Using pattern (3), cut three sepals. Vein with a corn husk and place in position.

Step 4: Take a piece of modelling paste and roll out thinly. Using pattern (4), cut two petals, frill the edges and attach to the sepals.

Step 5: Moisten the throat and firmly push into the centre. Allow to dry completely before colouring.

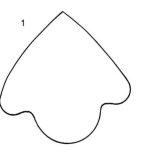
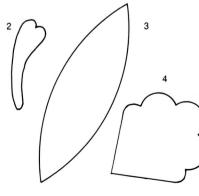

Orchid, Vanda

Vanda spp.

Colours: various

Step 1: Take a piece of modelling paste and hollow out to form a cone. Place on to a length of medium gauge wire for the column (1). Allow to dry.

Step 2: Take a piece of modelling paste and roll out thinly. Using pattern (2), cut one piece for the throat. Using scissors, make a cut on either side. Frill the front edge.

Step 3: Moisten the centre and attach to the cone. Allow to dry.

Step 4: Take a piece of modelling paste and roll out thinly. Using pattern (3), cut three sepals.

Step 5: Take a piece of modelling paste and roll out thinly. Using pattern (4), cut two wing petals. Vein all the petals and curve the top sepal and wing petals into the centre and the lower petals away from the centre.

Step 6: Secure in position with eggwhite.

Step 7: Insert the dry throat. Allow to dry before colouring.

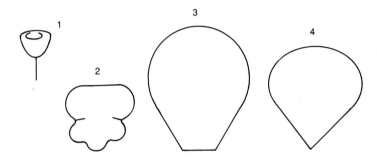

Orchid, Zygo

Zygopetalum spp.

Colours: various

Step 1: Take a small ball of modelling paste and insert a length of medium gauge hooked wire.

Step 2: Cut in half and then one side in quarters. Pull these two quarters to make the lobes of the tongue. Take the half and flatten with the thumb and pinch in the centre to cup up. Using tweezers, pinch each side of the tongue together (1).

Step 3: Take a piece of modelling paste and roll out. Using pattern (2), cut one throat leaving the centre thick enough to take wire. Finger the edges, vein and frill, insert the wire and allow to dry flat.

Step 4: Take a piece of modelling paste and roll out. Using pattern (3), cut three top petals and two side petals (4) leaving the centres thick enough to insert the wires. Finger the edges, insert the wire and drape in a slight curve and allow all pieces to completely dry before assembling.

Step 5: Colour each petal as desired.

Step 6: Securely tape the tongue and throat together.

Step 7: Place the three top petals in position. Then the two side petals and lastly place the tongue and throat in position taping all together securely.

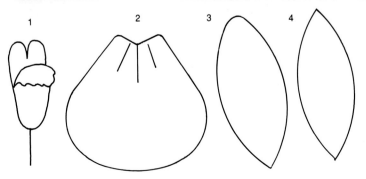

Oxalis

Oxalis spp.

Colours: pink

Pulled method

Step 1: Take a small ball of modelling paste and shape into a teardrop (1).

Step 2: Flatten the top and, using scissors, make five evenly spaced cuts around the top (2).

Step 3: Use the thumb and forefinger to round out and flatten each petal.

Step 4: Push a grooved modelling tool into the centre to mark.

Step 5: Push a length of fine gauge hooked wire into the centre and firm. Twist each gently and allow to dry.

Step 6: Touch the centre of the flower with lemon colour and paint the petals a deep shade of pink.

Pansy

Viola spp.

Colours: various

Cutter method

Step 1: Take a piece of modelling paste and roll out thinly. Using pattern (1), cut two pieces.

Step 2: Finger the edges, place on foam and ball in the centre. Allow to dry.

Step 3: Take a piece of modelling paste and roll out thinly. Using pattern (2), cut two pieces.

Step 4: Finger the edges, place on foam and ball in the centre. Allow to dry.

Step 5: Take a piece of modelling paste and roll out thinly. Using pattern (3), cut one piece.

Step 6: Finger the edges, place on foam and ball in the centre turning the point backwards. Allow to dry.

Step 7: Colour all petals. Place a small amount of royal icing in a shallow drying stand and place the petals in position.

Step 8: Pipe a yellow dot in the centre of the flower. Allow to dry.

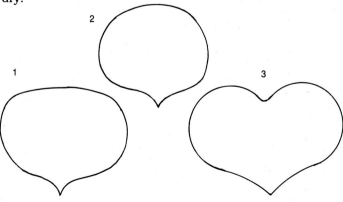

Alternate method:

Step 1: Take a small ball of modelling paste and finger out to

a petal shape (1). Trim with scissors if required making sure it is very fine on the edges. Place in palm of the hand and gently cup the petal. Allow to dry.

Step 2: Repeat step 1 four times.

Step 3: Paint all petals in the desired colours and allow to dry before arranging in royal icing.

Step 4: Pipe a yellow dot in the centre of the flower.

Pelargonium

Pelargonium spp.

Colours: various

Step 1: Take a piece of modelling paste and roll out thinly. Using pattern (1), cut a calyx. Place in a deep drying stand.

Step 2: Take a piece of modelling paste and roll out thinly. Using pattern (2), cut two petals. Vein and gently flute the edges. Moisten and place in the calyx with one petal overlapping the other.

Step 3: Take a piece of modelling paste and roll out thinly. Using pattern (3), cut three petals. Vein and gently flute the edges. Moisten the lower edge and place in the calyx as shown (4).

Step 4: Insert a cluster of eight finely curved stamens into the dampened centre of the flower. Allow to dry.

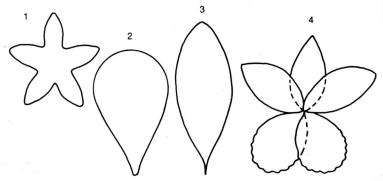

Petunia

Petunia X

Colours: various

Step 1: Take a large ball of modelling paste and hollow out to form a cone (1).

Step 2: Flatten the top and frill the edge with a cocktail stick (2).

Step 3: Mark the centre with a grooved modelling tool and insert a length of medium gauge wire and allow to dry in a flower stand.

Step 4: Paint the centre a golden yellow.

Step 5: Add a little royal icing and insert several short lemon stamens.

Step 6: Paint the outside and top edge the required colour.

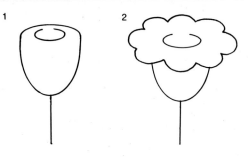

Pine Cones

Pinus spp.

Colours: brown, green

Step 1: Take a medium-sized ball of modelling paste and roll between the fingers to make a teardrop (1).

Step 2: Using fine, sharp scissors cut v-shaped serrations all round the cone. Make a second row of cuts, alternating the cuts between the lower ones. Continue until the whole shape is covered with cuts (2). Allow to dry.

Step 3: Paint the cone with brown colouring and arrange in clusters using green stamen cottons to represent the pine needles.

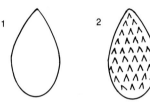

Plumbago

Capensis spp.

Colours: blue

Step 1: Take a small ball of modelling paste and hollow out to form a cone (1).

Step 2: Make five deep evenly spaced cuts around the top of the cone and insert a length of medium gauge hooked wire into the centre.

Step 3: Ease the paste down the wire to form the back of the flower (2).

Step 4: Flatten each petal between the fingers. Lightly flute and thin each petal with a modelling tool.

Step 5: Vein the centre of each petal with a sharp tool.

Step 6: Push a grooved modelling tool into the centre, then add a lemon stamen. Allow to dry.

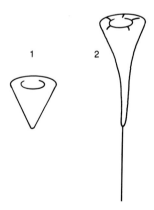

Poinsettia

Euphorbia spp.

Colours: pink, red, cream/yellow

Step 1: Take a piece of modelling paste and roll out very thinly. Using pattern (1), cut twelve large petals. Vein and twist each petal. Allow to dry before painting.

Step 2: Take a piece of modelling paste and roll out very thinly. Using pattern (2), cut ten medium petals. Vein and twist each petal. Allow to dry before painting.

Step 3: Take a piece of modelling paste and roll out very thinly. Using pattern (3), cut eight small petals. Vein and twist each petal. Allow to dry before painting.

Step 4: Take a piece of modelling paste and roll out very thinly. Using pattern (4), cut six tiny petals. Vein and twist each petal. Allow to dry before painting.

Step 5: Using green modelling paste make eight to ten small cups for the centre. Allow to dry, then paint the outside of each red. Paint the rims with eggwhite and dip into yellow pollen.

Step 6: Assemble the flower in royal icing, beginning with the largest petals, adding enough petals in each row to form a circle.

Step 7: When the rows are completed, cover the centre with the small cups. Allow to dry.

Poppy

Papaver spp.

Colours: various

Step 1: Take a medium-sized ball of green modelling paste and flatten the top (1). Insert a length of heavy gauge wire up through the base.

Step 2: Mark the top by pinching with tweezers (2).

Step 3: Paint the top with eggwhite and dip into yellow pollen.

Step 4: Paint the sides with eggwhite and cover with very finely crushed dry tea leaves. Allow to dry.

Step 5: Surround the dry centre with corn silk. Tie firmly.

Step 6: Take a piece of modelling paste and roll out thinly. Using pattern (3), cut four petals and keep covered.

Step 7: Take a square of aluminium foil and make 6 mm (1/4 inch) fand folds across it. Holding each end push to the middle to crush the foil. Gently ease out and use to vein the petals. Frill the edges and place as shown (4) in a shallow drying stand lined with foil.

Step 8: Push the centre through and allow to dry.

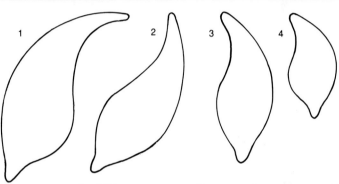

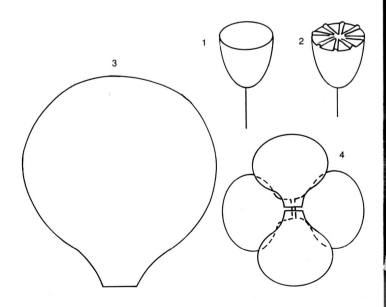

Portulaca

Portulaca spp.

Colours: various

Step 1: Tape fine stamens to a length of medium gauge wire.

Step 2: Take a small ball of modelling paste and make a Mexican hat (see page 12). Using pattern (1), cut one flower.

Step 3: Lightly frill the edge of each petal and place on foam. Using a small balling tool, bounce to cup each petal.

Step 4: Place a balling tool in the centre of the flower and bounce again.

Step 5: Pull the stamens into position. Allow to dry before painting.

Step 6: Make the phyllodes (see page 12).

Potato Flower

Solanum spp.

Colours: mauve, white

Step 1: Attach a small ball of modelling paste to a length of medium gauge wire. Shape to form a teardrop.

Step 2: Using tweezers, pinch grooves around it to form the centre. Add a small green stamen head to the top (1). Allow to dry. Dampen and dip into pollen.

Step 3: Take a piece of modelling paste and roll out thinly. Using pattern (2), cut one piece. Pinch the sides of each petal (3).

Step 4: Place on foam and bounce the centre, using a balling tool.

Step 5: Place the dry centre into the dampened middle of the petals. Allow to dry.

  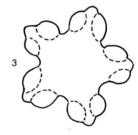

Primula

Primula spp.

Colours: various

Pulled method

Step 1: Take a small ball of modelling paste and hollow out to form a cone (1).

Step 2: Make five long evenly spaced cuts into the top and then make a small cut between each long cut (2).

Step 3: Using the thumb and index finger, gently pull each section between the long cuts from underneath while flattening the top with the thumb (3).

Step 4: Insert a length of fine gauge wire and reshape the centre with the rounded end of a modelling tool. Allow to dry.

Primula, Alpine Mountain

Primula spp.

Colours: shell pink

Pulled method

Step 1: Take a small ball of soft white modelling paste and shape into a teardrop (1).

Step 2: Flatten the top and, using scissors, make five evenly spaced cuts around the top (2).

Step 3: Pull one side of each cut, then the other side making heart-shaped petals (3).

Step 4: Insert a modelling tool (4) into the centre to make the throat.

Step 5: Place in a drying rack and allow the petals to fall flat. Allow to dry.

Step 6: When dry, colour the throat with a small amount of green colour. Paint or chalk the petals a soft shell pink, leaving a small area around the throat white.

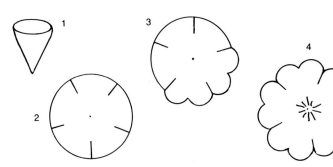

Protea

Protea spp.

Colours: pink, white

Cutter method

Step 1: Take a small teardrop-shaped piece of modelling paste and insert a length of heavy gauge hooked wire (1) and allow to dry. Or, wind sewing thread around the fingers until the required thickness. Secure with a length of heavy gauge wire.

Step 2: Take a piece of white modelling paste and roll out thinly. Using pattern (2), cut out one petal piece. Cut along each petal to give a spiked effect (3).

Step 3: Dampen the petal piece and attach to the dry centre arranging the cut edges evenly around the centre. Allow to dry.

Step 4: Dip the petal points in deep pink chalk.

Step 5: Take a piece of pale pink modelling paste and roll out thinly. Again using pattern (2), cut out another petal piece. Vein and ball up on foam. Attach to the dry centre. Allow to dry.

Step 6: Take a piece of white modelling paste and roll out thinly. Again using pattern (2), cut two more petal pieces. Vein and ball up on foam. Tint the centre with green colouring.

Step 7: Dampen and attach to the centre with the petals alternating. Allow to dry.

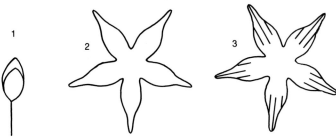

Ranuncula

Ranunculus spp.

Colours: various

Step 1: Wire together corn silks or cotton with a length of medium gauge wire. Moisten the top of the silks and dip in yellow pollen.

Step 2: Take a piece of modelling paste and roll out thinly. Using pattern (1), cut a calyx. Place in position in a flower stand and moisten with eggwhite.

Step 3: Take a piece of modelling paste and roll out thinly. Using pattern (2), cut three outer petals. Frill the edges and place in position on the calyx.

Step 4: Take a piece of modelling paste and roll out thinly. Using pattern (2), cut three more petals. Frill the edges, moisten the back and place in the centre of the other petals.

Step 5: Take a piece of modelling paste and roll out thinly. Using pattern (3), cut three inner petals. Frill the edges, moisten the back and place in the centre of the other petals.

Step 6: Moisten the flower centre and push the corn silks into position. Allow to dry.

Rose, Briar

Rosa spp.

Colours: various

Step 1: Take a small ball of yellow modelling paste and attach to a length of medium gauge hooked wire. Allow to dry.

Step 2: Dampen with eggwhite or gum glue and cover with yellow pollen. Redampen the edge and dip into brown pollen. Allow to dry.

Step 3: Firmly tape fine stamens or corn silks to the centre.

Step 4: Take a piece of modelling paste and roll out thinly. Using pattern (1), cut one petal. Thin the edges with your fingers, making sure the edges are very fine.

Step 5: Place the petal in the palm of the hand and press firmly to flute the edge, then place over the cushion of the thumb and gently pull the petal backwards.

Step 6: Repeat steps 4 and 5 for five petals. Allow to dry.

Step 7: Place a small amount of royal icing on a circle of waxed paper. Arrange the petals overlapping, making sure the last petal is tucked under the first.

Step 8: Pull the wired centre into position. Allow to dry.

90

Rose, Bridal

Colours: various

Step 1: Take a small ball of modelling paste and form a centre bud (1) on a length of medium gauge wire. Allow to dry.

Step 2: Take a piece of modelling paste and roll out thinly. Using pattern (2), cut three tiny petals. Wrap them around the bud to fully enclose it. Allow to dry.

Step 3: Take a piece of modelling paste and roll out thinly. Using pattern (3), cut three petals. Finger and frill the edges before attaching to the bud centre.

Step 4: Take a piece of modelling paste and roll out thinly. Using pattern (4), cut five petals. Finger and frill the edges. Assemble the petals in an outer row and turn back. Allow to dry.

Step 5: Take a piece of green modelling paste and roll out thinly. Using pattern (5), cut a calyx. Dampen and attach at the base of the rose.

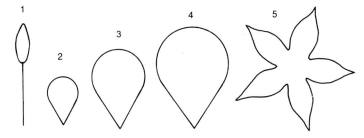

Rose, Camellia

Rosa spp.

Colours: various

Step 1: Take a large ball of modelling paste and make a long cone (1).

Step 2: Pinch one side of the cone to form a petal (2) and wrap around the remaining cone (3).

Step 3: Take a small piece of modelling paste and finger out to a petal shape (4). Attach to the cone trunk and turn the top edge of the petal slightly outwards.

Step 4: Continue to make petals and attach to the trunk until the centre is completed. (Approximately three rows.)

Step 5: Cut off the base and allow to dry thoroughly.

Step 6: Take a piece of modelling paste and roll out thinly. Using pattern (5), cut approximately fifteen petals. Finger and thin the edges. Cup on foam and turn the edges backwards. Allow to dry.

Step 7: Set an outside row of petals in a ring of royal icing then arrange another row inside these petals. Add more petals and royal icing then add the dry centre.

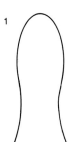
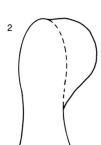

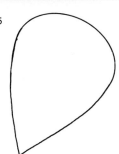

91

Rose, Cecil Brunner

Rosa spp.

Colours: pale pink

Step 1: Attach a tiny ball of modelling paste to a length of medium gauge hooked wire (1). Allow to dry.

Step 2: Take a very tiny piece of modelling paste and finger out finely to a petal shape. Moisten and attach to the dry centre to completely enclose the bud (2).

Step 3: Continue in this manner increasing the petal size until the rose is the desired size and shape. Gradually turn the top edge of the petals backwards (3). Allow to dry.

Step 4: Add a calyx (4).

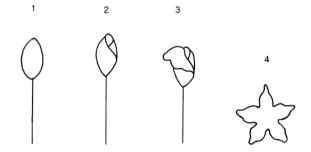

Rose, Christmas

Rosa spp.

Colours: white/red

Step 1: Take a small piece of modelling paste and finger out to a petal shape (1). Thin out with the fingers making sure it is very fine on the edges.

Step 2: Using scissors trim the petal to the correct shape if necessary. After trimming, finger the cut edges again.

Step 3: Place the petal in the palm of the hand and press gently to slightly curve the top edge. Allow to dry.

Step 4: Repeat steps 1–3, until you have five petals.

Step 5: Paint the back of each petal with a rich red. Allow to dry.

Step 6: Place a small amount of royal icing on a circle of waxed paper in a patty pan. Arrange the petals overlapping, making sure the last petal is tucked under the first.

Step 7: Insert stamens into the royal icing in the centre of the flower. Sprinkle with coloured pollen.

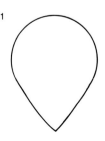

Rose, Dainty

Colours: various

Step 1: Attach a small ball of modelling paste to a length of medium gauge hooked wire (1). Allow to dry.

Step 2: Take a small piece of modelling paste and finger out to a petal shape (2). Moisten the petal with water and completely wrap around the bud.

Step 3: Take a small piece of modelling paste and finger out to a petal shape (2). Moisten across the base only and attach to the centre turning the top edge backwards.

Step 4: Repeat step 3 twice to completely enclose the centre. Allow to dry.

Step 5: Take a piece of modelling paste and roll out thinly. Using pattern (3), cut a calyx. Attach to the base of the flower.

Rose, Dog

Rosa spp.

Colours: various

Step 1: Take a small piece of modelling paste and finger out to a petal shape (1). Thin out, making sure it is very fine on the edges.

Step 2: Using scissors, trim the petal to the correct shape if necessary. After trimming, finger the edges again.

Step 3: Place the petal in the palm of the hand and press firmly to curve the top edge. Allow to dry.

Step 4: Repeat steps 1–4 to make five petals.

Step 5: Place a small amount of royal icing on a circle of waxed paper in a patty pan. Arrange the petals overlapping, making sure the last petal is tucked under the first petal.

Step 6: Cover the royal icing in the centre of the flower with stamens or pollen.

Step 7: To make the bud, take a piece of modelling paste and roll out thinly. Using pattern (2), cut three petals. Finger and thin the edges. Place each petal in the palm of the hand and press firmly to curve the top edge. Allow to dry. Assemble in royal icing and add a calyx if required.

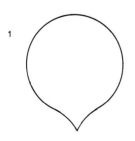

Rose, Double Dog

Rosa spp.

Colours: various

Step 1: Take a small piece of modelling paste and thin out with the fingers to form a petal (1) making sure it is very fine on the edges.

Step 2: Using scissors, trim the petal to the correct shape if necessary. After trimming, finger the cut edges again to smooth.

Step 3: Place the petal in the palm of the hand and press firmly to curve the top edge. Allow to dry.

Step 4: Repeat steps 1–3 to make four petals (1) then repeat steps 1–3 again to make five large petals (2). Allow to dry.

Step 5: Place some royal icing on a piece of waxed paper in a patty pan. Arrange the large petals overlapping, making sure last petal is tucked under the first petal.

Step 6: Place the smaller petals inside and finish the centre with stamens or coloured pollen.

Note: Tiffany rose can be made using the above instructions and patterns (3) and (4).

Rose, Formal

Rosa spp.

Colours: various

Step 1: Mix up at least three shades of modelling paste in the colour required.

Step 2: Take a large ball of modelling paste in the darkest shade and shape into a long cone (1). Completely cover the top of the cone with stamens to form the trunk.

Step 3: Take a small piece of modelling paste in the darkest shade and finger out to form a petal. Moisten and attach to the trunk (2).

Step 4: Continue to make petals and attach them to the trunk until the required size and shape is achieved, gently lightening each row of petals.

Step 5: Cut off the base and allow to dry thoroughly before using.

Step 6: To make the bud, take a medium-sized ball of modelling paste and shape into a cone. Pinch a petal from one side of the cone (3) and wrap around the cone (4).

Step 7: Cut off the base and attach a calyx.

94

Rose, Queen Elizabeth

Rosa spp.

Colours: pink

Step 1: Mix up at least three shades of modelling paste in the colour required.

Step 2: Take a large ball of the darkest modelling paste and shape into a long cone (1).

Step 3: Pinch one side of the cone to form a petal (2) and wrap around the cone (3).

Step 4: Take a small piece of the darkest modelling paste and finger out into a petal shape.

Step 5: Attach the petal to the cone trunk, turning the top edge of the petal slightly outwards (4).

Step 6: Continue to make petals and attach to the trunk gradually increasing the size and number of the petals and lightening the shade in each row until the required size and shape is achieved.

Step 7: Cut off the base and allow to dry thoroughly before using.

Step 8: To make the bud, take a piece of modelling paste and repeat steps 1 and 2. Cut off the base and attach a calyx (5).

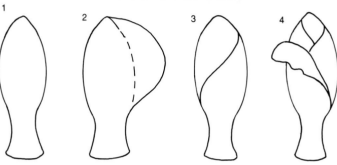

Rose, Tea

Rosa spp.

Colours: various

Step 1: Mix up at least three shades of modelling paste in the colour required.

Step 2: To make a centre bud, take a tiny ball of the darkest modelling paste and attach to a length of medium gauge wire. Allow to dry.

Step 3: Take a piece of the darkest modelling paste and roll out thinly. Using pattern (1), cut three tiny petals and completely enclose the bud. Allow to dry.

Step 4: Take a piece of medium shade modelling paste and roll out thinly. Using pattern (2), cut five petals, frilling the top of each. Attach to the bud centre.

Step 5: Take a piece of lighter shade modelling paste and roll out thinly. Using pattern (3), continue to add petals gradually lightening the shade in each row until the rose is the required shape and size. After each additional row, open the petals further and turn back. Allow to dry.

Step 6: Take a piece of modelling paste and roll out thinly. Using pattern (4), cut a calyx. Dampen and attach to the base of the rose.

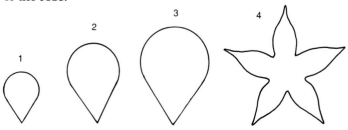

Rose, Three Petal

Rosa spp.

Colours: various

Step 1: Take a small ball of modelling paste and finger out flat. Thin the top edge and leave the centre thicker. Dampen the thick section and roll around a length of medium gauge hooked wire (1) leaving one end open to form the first petal (2).

Step 2: Take a piece of modelling paste and finger out to form two small petals (3). Attach to the centre on each side. Allow to dry.

Step 3: Attach or paint on a small calyx.

Step 4: To make the bud, repeat step 1.

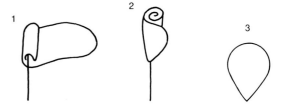

Rose, Triple Dog

Rosa spp.

Colours: various

Step 1: Mix up three shades of modelling paste in the colour required.

Step 2: For the centre row of petals, take a small piece of the darkest shade and finger out to form a petal (1). Neaten with scissors if required. Place in the palm of the hand and, using your finger, gently press the petal in the middle to curve the top. Make four petals.

Step 3: For the second row of petals, take a piece of the medium shade and finger out to form a petal (2). Trim and curve as for the smaller petals. Make five petals.

Step 4: For the third row of petals, take a piece of the lightest shade and finger to form a petal (3). Place in the palm of the hand and curl then place over the thumb and turn the top edge and sides backwards. Make seven petals.

Step 5: Allow all petals to completely dry.

Step 6: Pipe a large amount of royal icing on a piece of waxed paper in a patty pan. Arrange the seven outer petals in a circle. Arrange the second row of petals ensuring each petal overlaps the next. Arrange the smaller petals inside again. Place yellow and brown stamens or coloured pollen over the remaining royal icing. Allow to dry.

Rose of Sharon

Hypericum spp.

Colours: yellow

Step 1: Wind sewing thread over the fingers until the required thickness. Secure with a length of medium gauge wire through the centre (1).

Step 2: Cut the cottons, trim and then paint the ends with eggwhite and dip into coloured pollen.

Step 3: Take a piece of green modelling paste and roll out thinly. Using pattern (2), cut a calyx. Moisten and place in the centre of a deep flower ring.

Step 4: Take a piece of lemon modelling paste and roll out thinly. Using pattern (3), cut five petals. Vein and frill the edges. Place on foam and gently bounce the petals.

Step 5: Place the petals in position on the moistened calyx.

Step 6: Pull the prepared cottons through the moistened flower centre.

Step 7: Take a tiny ball of modelling paste and mould into a tiny teardrop. Push a pointed stamen head into the top (4). Moisten the back and place in the centre of the cottons. Allow to dry.

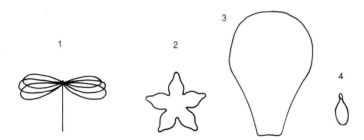

Sage, Blue

Salvia spp.

Colours: blue, purple, red

Step 1: Attach a tiny ball of modelling paste to a length of fine gauge hooked wire (1). Allow to dry.

Step 2: Take a piece of modelling paste and roll out thinly. Using pattern (2), cut one piece.

Step 3: Thin the edge and frill the front petal for the throat.

Step 4: Moisten and attach to the bud, pulling forwards. Allow to dry (3).

Step 5: Dip the whole flower into food colouring and allow to dry before painting or piping white lines onto the throat.

Snowdrop

Galanthus spp.

Colours: white

Pulled method

Step 1: Take a small ball of modelling paste and hollow out to form a cone. Make six short evenly spaced cuts around the edge (1).

Step 2: Mitre or pull each section into a petal shape (2). Using a small balling tool, thin and cup each petal.

Step 3: Push a length of fine gauge hooked wire through the centre keeping the base of the flower rounded. Allow to dry.

Step 4: Attach a tiny ball of green modelling paste by threading along the wire to the back of the dried flower or pipe a small dot of royal icing on the back of the flower.

Step 5: Paint a small green dot on each petal.

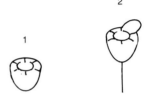

Solomon's Seal

Polygonatum spp.

Colours: white/green

Step 1: Take a small ball of modelling paste and push onto a pointed tool to thin to a long tube.

Step 2: Make six very shallow evenly spaced cuts into the top edge (1).

Step 3: Mitre each section and thin to form a petal.

Step 4: Reshape on a modelling tool and insert a length of fine gauge wire.

Step 5: Arrange the petals and allow to dry.

Step 6: Paint the base of the flower green.

Stephanotis

Stephanotis spp.

Colours: creamy white

Pulled method

Step 1: Take a small ball of modelling paste and shape into a long thin cone. Flatten the top and make five evenly spaced cuts around the top edge (1).

Step 2: Gently flatten and pinch each petal to shape.

Step 3: Using a modelling tool, thin the petals and insert a length of fine gauge wire.

Step 4: Gently thin the back of the flower down the wire. Allow to dry.

Sturt's Desert Pea

Clianthus spp.

Colours: red, purple

Step 1: Take a small ball of modelling paste and attach to a length of medium gauge hooked wire. Shape into a teardrop and flatten (1). Allow to dry.

Step 2: Take a piece of modelling paste and roll out thinly. Using pattern (2), cut one base petal. Moisten the back and fold in half around the dry centre. Curve the bottom gently forward (3).

Step 3: Take a piece of modelling paste and roll out thinly. Using pattern (4), cut one piece. Cut down the centre to form two wings. Moisten and attach one wing on either side of the base petal (5).

Step 4: For the boss, take a small ball of modelling paste and attach over the top of the wings. Mark the centre (6). Allow to dry.

Step 5: Take a piece of modelling paste and roll out thinly. Using pattern (7), cut one keel. Pinch along the centre, moisten the rounded end and attach over the top of the boss. Gently ease the pointed head open. Allow to dry.

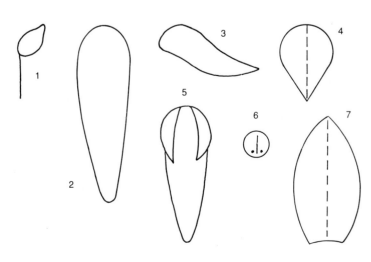

Sweet Pea

Lathyrus spp.

Colours: various

Cutter method

Step 1: Attach a small ball of modelling paste to a length of medium gauge hooked wire. Flatten and bend slightly backwards for the pea (1). Allow to dry.

Step 2: Take a piece of modelling paste and roll out thinly. Using pattern (2), cut one petal and thin the edges.

Step 3: Moisten and attach to the pea, completely enclosing it. Allow to dry.

Step 4: Take a piece of modelling paste and roll out thinly. Using pattern (2), cut one petal. Thin the edges and frill. Moisten down the centre only and attach to the pea. Allow to dry.

Step 5: Take a piece of modelling paste and roll out thinly. Using pattern (3), cut a third petal. Finger the edges and frill. Moisten down the centre only and attach to the pea, turning this petal outwards. Allow to dry before colouring and attaching a calyx.

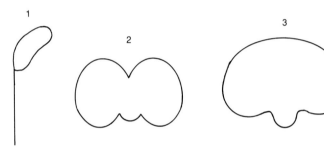

Sweet Rocket

Colours: various

Cutter method

Step 1: Take a tiny ball of modelling paste and shape into teardrop.

Step 2: Make four deep cuts in the shape of a cross across the top (1).

Step 3: Using a pointed modelling tool place in the middle of the cross and gently pull each section across your index finger (2) to lengthen the petals.

Step 4: Moisten the head of a stamen and insert into the centre of the flower (3). Lift the petals if required (4).

Tree Tulip

Colours: various

Step 1: Take a medium-sized ball of green modelling paste and attach to a length of medium gauge hooked wire. Shape into a long sausage (1).

Step 2: Using tweezers, pinch five grooves around the top (2). Paint the top with eggwhite and dip into yellow pollen. Allow to dry.

Step 3: Take a piece of modelling paste and roll out. Using pattern (3), cut six petals leaving the centre of each thick enough to insert a wire. Vein both sides and place into a curved drying stand. Allow to dry.

Step 4: Assemble the flower by arranging three petals around the centre with the three remaining petals forming an outer layer. Tape all petals together.

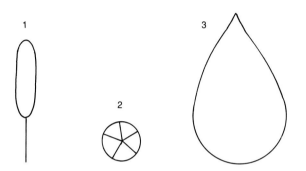

Tuberose

Polianthes spp.

Colours: cream

Cutter method

Step 1: Take a tiny ball of lemon modelling paste and make a bud on a piece of medium gauge wire (1). Using tweezers, pinch grooves around the side. Allow to dry.

Step 2: Take a piece of modelling paste and roll out thinly. Using cutter (2), cut one shape. Finger the edges to thin. Attach to the dry centre.

Step 3: Take a piece of modelling paste and roll out thinly. Using cutter (3) cut one piece. Finger the edges to thin. Dampen with water and attach to the flower.

Step 4: Cut a third shape using cutter (4). Finger the edges to thin. Moisten and attach to the flower. Allow to dry.

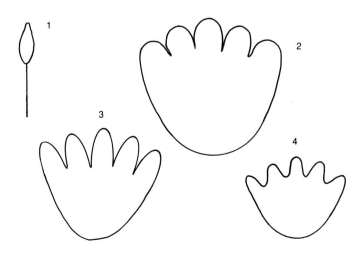

Valerian

Kentranthus spp.

Colours: mauve

Step 1: Attach fifteen to twenty very fine stamens to a length of medium gauge wire.

Step 2: Take a medium-size ball of modelling paste and make a Mexican hat (see page 12). Using pattern (1), cut one flower.

Step 3: Vein gently and place on foam. Using a balling tool, bounce the centre to cup the flower.

Step 4: Moisten the centre and insert stamens. Allow to dry.

1

Viburnum

Viburnum spp.

Colours: various

Step 1: Take a tiny ball of modelling paste and hollow out. Make five evenly spaced cuts around the top (1).

Step 2: Mitre each petal and, using a modelling tool, thin the cut edges.

Step 3: Insert a length of fine gauge hooked wire through the back of the flower and secure in position.

Step 4: Add three to five very fine stamens to the centre of the flower. Allow to dry.

1

Viola

Viola spp.

Colours: pink, mauve

Pulled method

Step 1: Take a small ball of modelling paste and flatten the top. Make five evenly spaced cuts around the top (1).

Step 2: Insert a length of medium gauge hooked wire into the centre and firm.

Step 3: Point and pull the two top petals and the two side petals.

Step 4: Using the thumb and index finger, round and thin the throat petal pulling gently from underneath.

Step 5: Insert a single yellow stamen into the centre and allow to dry (2).

Step 6: Paint the edges of the petals with pink-mauve alcohol wash, leaving the centre area white. Add fine black lines to the throat area.

Violet

Viola spp.

Colours: white, pink, mauve

Cutter method

Step 1: Take a small ball of modelling paste and roll between the fingers to form a cone shape. Flatten the top.

Step 2: Hollow out finely with a straight modelling tool and make five cuts around the top (1).

Step 3: Cut the top four petals to a point and round off the lower centre petal (2).

Step 4: Thin the edge of each petal to neaten.

Step 5: Insert a length of medium gauge hooked wire into the centre of the flower.

Step 6: Cup the rounded lower petal upwards. Turn the side petals outwards. Allow to dry.

Step 7: Using a slightly damp brush, paint with violet alcohol wash. Leave the centre of the flower white.

Step 8: When the paint is dry, brush on a green calyx using runny royal icing.

Step 9: Pipe a small dot of yellow royal icing in the centre.

Step 10: To finish the flower, paint fine black lines on the lower petal.

103

Violet

Viola spp.

Colours: white, pink, mauve

Pulled method

Step 1: Take a small ball of modelling paste and flatten one end. Make five cuts around the top (1).

Step 2: Insert a single yellow stamen into the centre. Allow to dry.

Step 3: Pull and point the top two petals and the side petals.

Step 4: Using the thumb and index finger, round and thin the throat petal pulling from underneath. Allow to dry.

Step 5: Paint with violet alcohol wash leaving the small area around the centre white.

1

Wandering Jew

Tradescantia spp.

Colours: white, mauve

Cutter method

Step 1: Tape some very fine stamens or corn silks to a length of medium gauge wire.

Step 2: Take a piece of modelling paste and roll out thinly. Using pattern (1), cut the flower.

Step 3: Vein the front of the petals, turn over and, using a fine pointed stick, mark a line down the centre o f each petal (2).

Step 4: Turn over and dampen the centre.

Step 5: Pull the wired stamens through the centre. Allow to dry.

Alternative method:

Step 1: Tape some very fine stamens to a length of medium gauge wire.

Step 2: Take a small ball of modelling paste and hollow out.

Step 3: Make three evenly spaced cuts around the top. Mitre each section to form a petal.

Step 4: Using a veining tool mark the petals.

Step 5: Dampen the centre and insert the wired stamens. Allow to dry.

1    2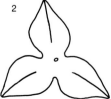

104

Waratah

Telopea spp.

Colours: red

Step 1: Colour a batch of modelling paste with strong red colour.

Step 2: Take a piece of the red modelling paste and roll out thinly. Using pattern (1), cut ten to twelve sepals. Wire, then vein with a corn husk. Drape to dry over cotton wool or in cornflour (cornstarch) box.

Step 3: Take a piece of modelling paste and using pattern (2) make sixteen of the smallest bracts on lengths of fine gauge wire, twenty-four of the next size, thirty of the next, forty-eight of the next, twenty-two of the next and forty-four of the largest. Allow to dry.

Step 4: Take a piece of modelling paste and roll out thinly. Using pattern (3) cut forty-four petals and add to the largest bracts. Turn the tops back. Allow to dry.

Step 5: Paint all parts with pillarbox red food colouring and allow to dry before assembling.

Step 6: Start assembling at the centre using the smallest bracts. Bind together with fine gauge wire. Gradually add all the bracts bending the wire outwards to keep the shape (4).

Step 7: When all the bracts are bound together add the sepals. Cut off the excess wire and cover with florist's tape.

Step 8: To complete the flower, colour the tips of the sepals and the top of the flower with a red/brown colour.

Note: This flower may also be made in white

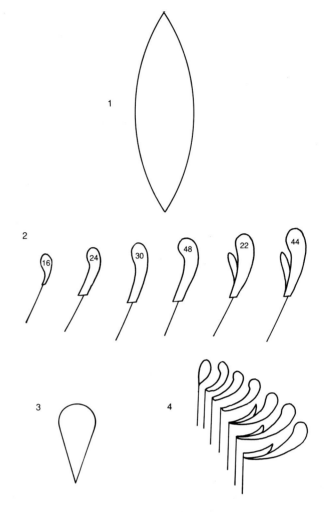

Waterlily

Nymphaea spp.

Colours: various

Step 1: Take a piece of modelling paste and roll out thinly. Using pattern (1) cut seven petals. Vein and ball up on foam. Allow to dry.

Step 2: Take a piece of modelling paste and roll out thinly. Using pattern (2) cut a waterlily pad. Place on foil.

Step 3: Take a piece of modelling paste and roll out thinly. Using pattern (3) cut eight petals. Vein and gently curve each petal and arrange on the moistened lily pad.

Step 4: Take a piece of modelling paste and roll out thinly. Using pattern (4) cut seven petals, vein and gently curve. Moisten the back and arrange over the outer row of petals making sure to alternate petals.

Step 5: Insert some stamens, then moisten the back of the dry centre petals and arrange, cupping over the stamens. Allow to dry.

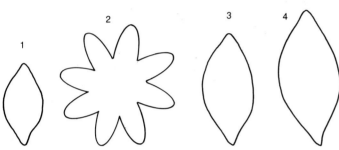

Waterlily Tulipa

Colours: various

Cutter method

Step 1: Make the pistil by rolling a small piece of modelling paste onto a length of medium gauge wire (1). Paint with eggwhite and dip into yellow sugar. Allow to dry.

Step 2: Tape some stamens under the pistil to form the flower centre.

Step 3: Take a ball of modelling paste and roll out thinly. Using pattern (2) cut two pieces. Finger the edges and vein.

Step 4: Place one piece in a drying stand, moisten the centre and place the second piece into position alternating the petals.

Step 5: Push the flower centre into position. Allow to dry.

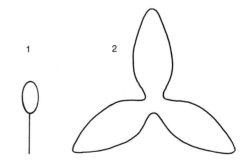

Watsonia

Watsonia spp.

Colours: orange

Step 1: Tape five stamens of various lengths to a length of medium gauge wire.

Step 2: Take a medium sized ball of yellow modelling paste and hollow out to form a cone shape (1).

Step 3: Make five evenly spaced cuts around the top of the

cone and mitre to form five pointed petals.

Step 4: Insert the stamens and allow to dry.

Step 5: Paint the petals with orange colouring.

Step 6: To make the buds, attach small pieces of modelling paste to a length of fine gauge wire. Gently curve the larger buds as shown.

Wattle or Acacia

Acacia spp.

Colours: yellow

Step 1: Take a small ball of yellow modelling paste and insert a length of fine gauge wire. Allow to dry. Moisten and dip into coloured sugar. Allow to dry.

Step 2: Mould tiny long buds onto fine gauge wire and allow to dry.

Step 3: To make leaves, take a piece of green modelling paste and roll into an elongated shape. Insert a length of fine gauge wire and flatten with the fingers. Mark a vein and allow to dry (1).

Wedding Bush

Ricinocarpus spp.

Colours: white

Step 1: Prepare a flower centre by tying lemon cottons or corn silks onto a length of medium gauge wire (1). Paint the tips with brown colouring.

Step 2: Take a small ball of modelling paste and hollow out to form a cone shape. Make five evenly spaced cuts around the top (2).

Step 3: Pinch and pull each section and thin using a small balling tool.

Step 4: Insert the wired cottons. Allow to dry.

Step 5: Twist short lengths of florist's tape to form the phyllodes needed to complete the spray (3).

107

Weigela

Weigela spp.

Colours: various

Pulled method

Step 1: Tape fine stamens to a length of medium gauge wire.

Step 2: Take a medium sized ball of modelling paste and roll into a teardrop shape. Flatten the top and hollow out.

Step 3: Make five evenly spaced cuts around the top (1)

Step 4: Pull each section from underneath and then gently frill to form a petal.

Step 5: Insert the wired stamens and allow to dry.

Wheat

Triticum spp.

Colours: yellow

Step 1: Thread a small ball of yellow modelling paste on to a length of stamen cotton. Leave the end of the cotton protruding (1). Groove either side with back of a craft knife. Allow to dry.

Note: You will need approximately thirty to make one head of wheat. When arranging add some corn silk between the wheat ears.

White Fabiana

Colours: white

Pulled method

Step 1: Take a tiny ball of white modelling paste and hollow out the centre (1).

Step 2: Make four evenly spaced cuts around the top (2). Pull each section from underneath to form broad petals.

Step 3: Curl the edge backwards and insert a length of fine gauge wire in the centre. Allow to dry.

Step 4: Dust the centre of the flower with yellow chalk and arrange in small clusters.

Step 5: To make the bud, take a small ball of modelling paste and mould onto a length of fine gauge wire.

108

White Pentas

Colours: white

Pulled method

Step 1: Take a small ball of modelling paste and shape into a long thin cone. Flatten the top and make five evenly spaced cuts around the top (1).

Step 2: Gently flatten and pinch each section to form a petal.

Step 3: Push a modelling tool into the flower centre to reshape. Insert a length of fine gauge hooked wire.

Step 4: Using sharp scissors cut a calyx in the back of the flower (2). Allow to dry.

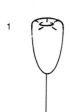 

Yesterday, Today and Tomorrow

Brunfelsia spp.

Colours: white, pink, blue, mauve

Cutter method

Step 1: Take a medium-sized ball of modelling paste and make a Mexican hat (see page 12). Using cutter (1), cut one flower shape.

Step 2: Using a fine modelling tool, roll and thin the edge of each petal, frilling slightly.

Step 3: Insert a heavy stamen or small daisy centre well down in the centre and twist the petals gently. Allow to dry.

Step 4: Paint the flowers in shades of pink and mauve. Leave some white.

Ziera

Ziera spp.

Colours: white

Pulled method

Step 1: Take a small ball of white modelling paste and hollow out to form a cone (1).

Step 2: Make four equal cuts around the top and about one quarter the depth of the cone (2).

Step 3: Pull each section gently from underneath to form a petal.

Step 4: Squeeze and pull the tops of the petals forward.

Step 5: Insert a length of medium gauge hooked wire and add three or four large red stamen heads. Allow to dry.

109

Equipment

Essential equipment used for the making of cake decorating flowers includes from top left: veiners, florists tape, cake decorating wire, pliers, rolling pins, modelling tools. scissors, scalpels and cutters.

The correct choice of drying stand is essential to produce flowers of the quality seen in this book. These include stands of varying sizes as well as items that you find around your kitchen such as foil rings, curtain rings, egg cups and ice ball trays.

Colours specially designed for cake decorating can be purchased at your local supplier. These should be marked non-toxic and include liquid colours for painting or air-brushing, chalks for brushing, Caketime pens as well as a selection of brushes.

Index

The numbers in *italics* refer to illustrations.
The numbers in **bold** refer to patterns.
The numbers for the flowers refer to the text, patterns and illustrations.